ONE TOUCH
FROM
THE KING . . .

'Once again Mark Stibbe has enlightened us and brought reality to truths that are all too often forgotten, overlooked, or historically dismissed. His book, *One Touch from the King . . . Changes Everything*, brings us to a place where we not only know of God's love, passion and power that is there for each of us, but we are carried towards a newness of faith that God actually longs to act on our behalf. Why read this book? Because, it will cause faith to explode in your heart.'
John Paul Jackson, Streams Ministries

'Rarely do you find a book that asks important questions, gives answers, shares living testimonies, and draws the reader to the scriptures. Mark has a wonderful gift of being an enquirer before the throne of God and coming back with the heart of God. *One Touch from the King* is one of the most satisfying yet challenging books I have read on healing and miracles.'
Revd Dr David E. Carr, Senior Minister Renewal Christian Centre, Solihull, England & Regional Overseer Free Methodist Church UK

'Mark Stibbe's book *One Touch from the King* shatters self-imposed limitations you might have placed on yourself, or have had placed on you by others. Mark Stibbe instructs and inspires us to believe the truth that Jesus the Great Physician is the same yesterday, today and forever. This book inspired me to believe, expect and act.'
Canon J. John, author and evangelist

'I'm really excited about this wonderful new book from Mark Stibbe. I found myself marking almost every paragraph on every page to go back to read again. I can honestly say that it has inspired and renewed me to ask for that One Touch from the King. This is a super book!'
Julie Sheldon, author of the best selling book, *Dancer off her Feet*

'*One Touch from the King* is a timely and much needed book. In the early church the saints knew and experienced the awesomeness of God in everyday life.

In too much of the ordinary church life of today, the extraordinary touch of God's hand of grace is highly conspicuous by its absence. Without the presence and power of God in our midst we fall short of experiencing the Kingdom of God that so radically affected the cultures of the first three centuries after Christ. Rather than proclaiming and demonstrating the Kingdom, we are often left merely rehashing and criticizing so-called critical doctrines and the traditions of man. Dr Mark Stibbe, like Luke, the "beloved physician", wonderfully utilises both testimonies and the Word of God to call us to a fresh appreciation of God in our midst, and power of his compassion for people in need. I believe this book to be both a wake-up call and a pointer towards where the church of the new millennium is heading.'
Mark A. Dupont, Mantle of Praise Ministries, December, 2006

ONE TOUCH
FROM
THE KING . . .

. . . CHANGES EVERYTHING

MARK   STIBBE

Authentic

LONDON ● ATLANTA ● HYDERABAD

First published 2007 by Authentic Media
9 Holdom Avenue, Bletchley, Milton Keynes, Bucks, MK1 1QR, UK
285 Lynnwood Avenue, Tyrone, GA 30290, USA
OM Authentic Media
Medchal Road, Jeedimetla Village, Secunderabad 500 055, A.P., India
www.authenticmedia.co.uk
Authentic Media is a division of Send the Light Ltd., a company limited
by guarantee (registered charity no. 270162)

British Library Cataloguing in Publication Data

A catalogue record for this book is available from the
British Library

ISBN 978-1-86024-597-8

Cover Design by Pete Goddard and fourninezero design.
Print Management by Adare Carwin
Printed and bound by J.H. Haynes & Co., Sparkford

This book is dedicated to Phil Clark
24 November 1931 – 12 December 2005

Contents

Just One Touch

Verse:

If you are desperate, I know
When hearts are broken, I care
There is no problem that I cannot solve
There is no sickness that I cannot heal

This is your moment; don't wait
This is your hour; press in
Only reach out; it's time to receive
Look to me now and only believe

Chorus:

Just one touch; just one moment in time
Just one touch brings your heart close to mine
Just one touch from your Master's hand –
Just one touch from the King changes everything

Just one touch, just one touch
Just one touch changes everything.

Hallelu, hallelu, hallelu, hallelujah

Foreword

'And she went, and came, and gleaned in the field after the reapers: and her hap was to light on a part of the field belonging unto Boaz, who was of the kindred of Elimelech.' 'And let fall also some of the handfuls on purpose for her, and leave them, that she may glean them, and rebuke her not' (Ruth 2:3,16, KJV).

There are two very interesting insights in the Book of Ruth that are intriguing to me, and they are interwoven; indeed, the second event in verse 16 is the by-product of the first event in verse 3. Ruth, in her noble desire to care for her grieving mother-in-law Naomi, sets out to find a place of employment that will produce favour. She 'happens' upon the field of Boaz – the one person qualified to be their redeemer. Boaz gives his workers instructions to be very intentional about providing an abundant but unearned harvest for Ruth.

I believe that Dr Mark Stibbe's ministry is characterized by the same dynamic, in that once he 'chances' upon a life-changing insight, he is diligent in his quest to understand and then impart what the Father has entrusted to him. And it is in these quests that the Father lets fall to him 'handfuls on purpose'.

Someone once said, 'Heroes are not born; they're cornered.' In the same vein, I am convinced that great truths, life-transforming truths, often 'happen' into our lives when we are simply too tired to reject them. Great insights can come to us in that strange state between sleeping and waking. These revelations are essentially unveilings that happen to us in unguarded moments when we are too tired to care or even argue, and the left-brain simply surrenders to an overwhelming insight without the usual fight. The outcome itself is amazing, and *we* are credited with undeserved brilliance because the Father wanted to get a simple truth to his children.

Mark's account in this book of his encounter with the carpenter Hank is a wonderful example of the gracious way the Father reveals his truths to us, and of course Mark's desire to steward this truth is indicative of the Father's concern that his gifts should be used to communicate those same truths with humility and brilliance.

In the fall of 2005 in Pittsburgh, Pennsylvania, at Covenant Church, Dr Mark Stibbe delivered this powerful message – that you can have what I call an 'elliptical encounter'. Now, in our church, you only have to say the words, 'Just one touch from the King . . .' and the immediate and enthusiastic response will be, '. . . changes everything!'

Great insights and great discoveries produce 'children', and one of the children of Dr Stibbe's message is a song that some of us wrote after he preached in Covenant in October 2005. The congregation now sings the truth of the sermon: 'Just one touch from the King changes everything.' That song is on a CD in this book.

Another 'child' is the amazing increase of the miraculous, particularly in my wife's healing ministry. Just a few days ago she prayed for a young woman who had cracked her funny bone in a fall. When she laid her hands upon the injured area, there was an immediate loud crack, and the pain was instantly gone! The following day, X-rays revealed that the bone was perfectly whole, and the specialist actually said, 'This is not the same arm I saw a few days ago.' Her employers, who had witnessed the accident, were simply astounded and promised her they would come to church.

This increase in the miraculous is another by-product. Dr Stibbe prophesied a release of greater faith in our house to believe for and to see the miraculous works of the King in our daily lives.

It is my prayer that those who read this book will be encouraged through precept and example that they too can produce more 'children', since we are convinced that the King himself wants to see his 'touch' multiplied in the life of every believer.

Bishop Joseph L. Garlington, Sr
Covenant Church of Pittsburgh
Pittsburgh, Pennsylvania, USA

Introduction

Just One Touch . . .

Sometimes something happens in your Christian life and it changes your world for ever. Sociologists call it a 'paradigm shift' – an intellectual revolution in which one way of viewing the world is replaced by another. Well, that's what I experienced not long ago. Let me describe it to you.

I was ministering in the States and had just finished the last message in a busy series of meetings. I was very tired and running on empty. A man came up to me while I was waiting for a car to take me to the restaurant. I was sipping coffee and not really wanting to talk, but he stretched out his hand and grabbed hold of mine. He then kept hold of it and told me his life story. He said his name was Hank, that he'd been a carpenter for thirty years; that he worked on a construction site, and a number of other things. To be honest, I was so exhausted I just nodded my head.

A few minutes after he had gone, a lady called Tina came up to me and said how amazing it was, what had happened to Hank. I said I didn't know what she was talking about. She then told me that he had come to church with a severe headache and that when he grabbed my hand, he felt power go into his hand, up his arm, through his shoulder and into his head. He said he had been instantly healed!

Now that got my attention, and for two reasons.

First, Hank was not a Christian and had come to church that morning at the request of his wife. A number of the church had been praying for some time that God would touch his life.

Secondly, because I felt absolutely nothing physically. I was completely empty spiritually. And I had a very bad attitude emotionally! So I knew it wasn't anything to do with me.

About an hour later I was taken to a restaurant. The pastor started to give thanks to the Lord about Hank. I then began to realise that this was a big deal for his church. As I registered that, the Holy Spirit started to speak to me about Hank's life and destiny. I had no paper handy so I wrote it down on a restaurant napkin. The word went something like this: 'Hank, just as Jesus had thirty years as a carpenter, so God has given you thirty years as a carpenter. Just as Jesus had a day of destiny when God touched his life in the River Jordan, so God has given you a day of destiny TODAY and touched your life. Just as Jesus went on to minister God's love to others, so God is calling you to take what you have received and to share it with others. Hank, this is the moment to turn your life over to God. Give him your heart.'

I gave that napkin to the lady next to me, a friend and prayer partner of Tina's. That evening she gave it to Tina, who then passed it on to Hank. One week later I received this amazing email from Tina, in which she described what happened next:

> I received your note to Hank on Monday morning. I placed it in a sealed envelope (I didn't read it) and put it on his desk in his office which is his first stop after he gets home at night. When he got home I told him about it and who it was from. Then I went upstairs and left him alone with the note. He came upstairs and couldn't believe you took the time to write to him after only meeting for a few minutes. He shared with me the contents of the note. As a matter of fact he placed it in a frame and put it on his desk.
>
> I want you to know that the Holy Spirit reached out and touched Hank through you. He is a different person. He has now come to know Jesus in a real and living way. He has changed dramatically in a short period of time. Already, since last Sunday, he has spoken to two different people about the fact that God touched his life, and how they can have what he has too.

I have personally heard from the wife of a guy that he works with and she said he cannot believe the changes in Hank at work. Hank has told me that people at the construction site are looking at him and asking what's happened. And he tells them – straight up! If someone would have told me a month ago that this was going to happen I would never have believed them.

And the best part is how he has been with our son. Today when he came home Hank just hugged him and said not to worry about things. Our son started crying. I could not believe what was happening.

God has captured my husband's heart and best of all he is already using it to touch others. I believe that what God gave Hank will be passed down into our family legacy for ever because of this.

As I read this email, I experienced a massive revolution in my thinking. I had simply shaken a man's hand, and his whole world had changed. I had felt nothing, yet God had done in a matter of hours the most extraordinary work of transformation. As I gave glory to God, a sentence came into my heart. Prompted no doubt by the references to God touching Hank's life in Tina's email, I sensed the Holy Spirit giving me a simple message that I have been sharing ever since:

'One Touch from the King Changes Everything!'

And everything did change for Hank.

His health was transformed.
His marriage was transformed.
His family was transformed.
His workplace was transformed.
His priorities were transformed.
His church was transformed.
EVERYTHING CHANGED for Hank.

Just one touch from the King . . . changes everything.
That's the message of this book.

It's a simple message. But we shouldn't be afraid of simplicity. Ralph Waldo Emerson once said that it is the task of the true educator to make hard things simple. Too often in the church, people make simple things hard. Jesus wasn't like that. Through puns, proverbs and parables he made hard things simple.

My message in this book is simply this: just one divine touch . . . that's all it takes.

God can radically transform your situation with just one royal touch. A moment of divine contact can bring an invasion of heaven into your world.

Of course I am aware that there are many who are still waiting and we will not evade the tough questions on the way, questions like, 'What happens when the King's touch is not experienced?' 'What happens when people are not healed and transformed instantly?' But my overriding desire is to encourage you to a new level of faith in the King's life-changing touch. My aim is to help raise your level of faith in the ability of the King of kings to touch your life.

There is nothing in the world quite like it.

As Plato once said, 'at the touch of a lover, everyone becomes a poet!'

Or as the songwriter put it,

When I feel the touch
Of your hand upon my life
It causes me to sing a song
That I love you, Lord.

Jesus is the Lover of your soul. Let him touch you through this book and let him change your world!

If Socrates entered the room,
we should rise and do him
honour. But if Jesus Christ
came into the room, we should
fall down on our knees and
worship him.

Napoleon Bonaparte

Chapter 1

The Hands of a King

This book is all about the power of 'the King's touch'. In the chapters that follow, you'll see that the King I'm referring to is Jesus, the King of kings. However, it's worth pointing out right at the beginning that the idea of 'the King's touch' has referred to other kings too.

The phrase 'royal touch' in fact has an ancient history. It goes back to the belief that the monarchs of England and France possessed the power to heal. During the Middle Ages, kings and queens were said to have divine power to heal various skin diseases and infections. In England this tradition began with Edward the Confessor, before the Norman Conquest in the eleventh century. It seems to have passed down from monarch to monarch until the death of Queen Anne in 1714. With the dawn of the eighteenth century – the Age of Reason – the belief died out.

Stories of royal healings are plentiful. King Charles II was perhaps the most prolific of the royal healers. John Brown, surgeon to St Thomas' Hospital and author of many learned works on surgery and anatomy, published accounts of sixty cures by the touch of this monarch. Sergeant-Surgeon Wiseman devotes an entire book to proving the reality of these healings, saying, 'I myself have been frequent witness to many hundreds of cures performed by his Majesty's touch alone without any assistance of surgery, and these many of them had tired out the endeavours of able surgeons before they came thither.'

Queen Elizabeth I was unafraid of touching even the worst skin disorders. She 'pressed the sores and ulcers' of patients and did so 'boldly and without disgust'. Queen Anne touched hundreds of sick people in large gatherings. Dr Daniel Turner in his *Art of Surgery* relates that several cases of skin disease which had been unsuccessfully treated by himself and other surgeons were healed by the Queen's touch.

Some monarchs regarded this 'gift' as superstition. William III is said on one occasion to have touched a sufferer with the words, 'God give you better health and more sense.' In spite of the King's scepticism, the man was healed.

The Church of England accepted the idea of the royal touch and included a special healing service in some editions of the Book of Common Prayer. When a monarch touched afflicted people, the attending bishop or priest recited the words, 'They shall lay their hands on the sick, and they shall recover.'

It was in the light of this tradition that J.R.R. Tolkien used this idea of the royal touch in *The Lord of the Rings*. In Middle Earth the Kings of Gondor – especially Aragorn – possess the power to heal. Indeed, one character says that 'the hands of a king are the hands of a healer'. Clearly the idea of the King's touch has a rich history.

The Ultimate Healer

Nowhere is this history richer than in the Gospels of Matthew, Mark and Luke, which describe the ministry of Jesus of Nazareth, whom nearly two billion people today worship as 'the King of kings'.

When it comes to 'the King's touch', there is no one quite like Jesus. He stands absolutely alone and unique as the King of all kings and the Lord of all lords. Even the great Elvis Presley, when he was called 'The King' (with the definite article), acknowledged that he was not worthy of that title. He replied, 'I am not a king. Christ is King.' Other great figures in history have recognised similar things both about their own limitations and Christ's unlimited greatness.

No less a person than Napoleon Bonaparte once famously remarked.

> Alexander, Caesar, Charlemagne and I have founded empires. But on what did we rest the creations of our genius? Upon force. Jesus Christ founded his empire upon love; and at this hour millions of men would die for him.

Jesus is supremely the King of kings, and during his three-year ministry two thousand years ago he frequently ministered what we might call 'the touch of the King'. Even in his own town, where he met a good deal of unbelief, many still recognised how special he was. In Mark 6 verse 2 we are told.

> And when the Sabbath had come, He began to teach in the synagogue. And many hearing Him were astonished, saying, 'Where did this Man get these things? And what wisdom is this which is given to Him, that such mighty works are performed by His hands!'

Notice the phrase, 'by his hands'. Jesus performed mighty works (that is, miracles, especially miracles of healing) through his hands. That means he touched those whom he prayed for. It also means that those he touched were healed.

Truly, one touch from the King changed everything.

A Royal Touch

Let's look at some examples of this royal touch in the life and ministry of Jesus. The passages can be found in Matthew, Mark and Luke and they can be grouped into three kinds of story: those which describe Jesus praying for the sick with the laying-on of hands; those that describe Jesus taking hold of someone's hand; and those that actually use the verb 'touch'.

Let's start with those passages that make reference to Jesus praying for the sick with the laying-on of hands:

Matthew 9:18 (see also Mark 5:23):
While He spoke these things to them, behold, a ruler came and worshipped Him, saying, 'My daughter has just died, but come and lay Your hand on her and she will live.'

Mark 6:5:
Now He could do no mighty work there, except that He laid His hands on a few sick people and healed them.

Mark 7:32:
Then they brought to Him one who was deaf and had an impediment in his speech, and they begged Him to put His hand on him.

Mark 8:23:
So He took the blind man by the hand and led him out of the town. And when He had spat on his eyes and put His hands on him, He asked him if he saw anything.

Mark 8:25:
Then He put His hands on his eyes again and made him look up. And he was restored and saw everyone clearly.

Luke 4:40:
When the sun was setting, all those who had any that were sick with various diseases brought them to Him; and He laid His hands on every one of them and healed them.

Luke 13:13:
And He laid His hands on her, and immediately she was made straight, and glorified God.

In every single one of these instances Jesus uses physical contact in his healing ministry. To be sure, there are a number of passages that show Jesus healing the sick using a word of command, and without touching the person. But in the references above, the laying-on of hands is the norm.

Now let's look at some passages where Jesus takes hold of the sick person as he ministers healing to them. In the few cases where we find this kind of description, Jesus is seen taking hold of the sufferer by the hand.

Mark 5:41–42 (see also Luke 8:54):
Then He took the child by the hand, and said to her, 'Talitha, cumi,' which is translated, 'Little girl, I say to you, arise.' Immediately the girl arose and walked, for she was twelve years of age. And they were overcome with great amazement.

Mark 9:27:
But Jesus took him by the hand and lifted him up, and he arose.

When the King Touches the Sick

Finally, let's look at those passages that use the Greek verb *haptomai*, meaning 'to touch'. There are 36 occasions in the New Testament when the verb 'touch' is used. Of these, 31 occur in Matthew, Mark and Luke. In 27 of these cases the verb *touch* is used in relation to miracles. We will look briefly at these now, beginning with stories in which Jesus touches the sick.

In Matthew, Mark and Luke, Jesus is seen stretching out his hand to touch the sick. In every case his touch produces a great miracle. This touch produces healing miracles in a whole variety of sicknesses and needs.

Fevers

One of the first miracles Jesus performed was the healing of Peter's mother-in-law. Matthew alone uses the verb 'touch' in his account of this miracle. In Matthew 8:14–15 we read:

Now when Jesus had come into Peter's house, He saw his wife's mother lying sick with a fever. So He **touched** her hand, and the fever left her. And she arose and served them.

While Mark and Luke do not use the verb 'touch', Matthew makes it clear that Jesus reached out to Peter's mother-in-law and touched her and that this touch resulted in instant healing. Here we see one touch from the King changing everything.

Leprosy

Another healing miracle involves one of the 'untouchables' in Jewish society, namely a leper. Mark says, 'Then Jesus, moved with compassion, stretched out His hand and **touched** him, and said to him, "I am willing; be cleansed"' (Mk. 1:41). Luke says, 'Then He put out His hand and **touched** him, saying, "I am willing; be cleansed." Immediately the leprosy left him' (Lk. 5:13). Matthew records the same moment in these words: 'Then Jesus put out His hand and **touched** him, saying, "I am willing; be cleansed." Immediately his leprosy was cleansed' (Mt. 8:3).

In all three of these accounts the same verb 'touch' is used, and in all three, one touch from the King changes everything.

Blindness

There are a number of examples of Jesus' touch healing the blind. In Matthew 20 Jesus meets two blind men. In verse 34 Matthew reports that 'Jesus had compassion and **touched** their eyes. And immediately their eyes received sight, and they followed Him.'

Mark has a similar episode in his Gospel. What is interesting is the fact that in Mark's account there is just one blind man and he is not healed instantly. Jesus touches his eyes twice and the healing comes gradually rather than instantly:

> Then He came to Bethsaida; and they brought a blind man to Him, and begged Him to **touch** him. So He took the blind man by the hand and led him out of the town. And when He had spat on his eyes and put His hands on him, He asked him if he saw anything. And he looked up and said, 'I see men like trees, walking.' Then He put His hands on his eyes again and made him look up. And he was restored and saw everyone clearly. Then He sent him away to his house, saying, 'Neither go into the town, nor tell anyone in the town.' (Mk. 8:22–26)

It is worth noting at this point that although John's Gospel does not use the word 'touch' for Jesus' healing miracles, there is an example of Jesus healing a blind man by making contact with his eyes. John records in 9:6–7:

> When He had said these things, He spat on the ground and made clay with the saliva; and He anointed the eyes of the blind man with the clay. And He said to him, 'Go, wash in the pool of Siloam' (which is translated, Sent). So he went and washed, and came back seeing.

Again, just one touch from the King changes everything.

Hearing and speech defects

Mark relates one incident involving Jesus touching deaf ears and a defective tongue. In Mark 7:31–35 we read:

> Again, departing from the region of Tyre and Sidon, He came through the midst of the region of Decapolis to the Sea of Galilee. Then they brought to Him one who was deaf and had an impediment in his speech, and they begged Him to put His hand on him. And He took him aside from the multitude, and put His fingers in his ears, and He spat and **touched** his tongue. Then, looking up to heaven, He sighed, and said to him, 'Ephphatha,' that is, 'Be opened.' Immediately his ears were opened, and the impediment of his tongue was loosed, and he spoke plainly.

Injuries

Luke records a remarkable incident in 22:50–51. At the scene of Jesus' arrest in the Garden of Gethsemane, one of the disciples uses his sword to cut off the ear of a servant:

> And one of them struck the servant of the high priest and cut off his right ear. But Jesus answered and said, 'Permit even this.' And He **touched** his ear and healed him.

Even at the time of Jesus' passion he is ministering healing – and in this case to his enemies! Even now one touch from the King changes everything.

Fear

The touch of the King is not restricted to physical healing. In Matthew 17:5–7 we see Jesus touching the three disciples who have accompanied him up the Mount of Transfiguration. Overwhelmed by fear, the disciples experience healing from an emotional need:

> While he was still speaking, behold, a bright cloud overshadowed them; and suddenly a voice came out of the cloud, saying, 'This is My beloved Son, in whom I am well pleased. Hear Him!' And when the disciples heard it, they fell on their faces and were greatly afraid. But Jesus came and **touched** them and said, 'Arise, and do not be afraid.'

The touch of the King changes not just physical disorders but emotional ones as well!

When the Sick Touch the King

You may have noticed in all the examples above that it is Jesus who takes the initiative in touching the sick. But there are also passages in Matthew, Mark and Luke where the sick touch Jesus. These incidents take one of two forms: they either describe an individual touching Jesus or depict crowds of sick people touching Jesus. Let's look briefly at examples of both.

Individuals

The most memorable story of an individual touching Jesus is the one with the woman who has a bleeding disorder – a disorder that she had endured for twelve years. Mark records this story in chapter 5 of his Gospel (verses 24–34) and uses the verb 'touch' four times. Matthew relates it in chapter 9 and uses the same verb three times. Luke's version reads as follows:

> Now a woman, having a flow of blood for twelve years, who had spent all her livelihood on physicians and could not be

healed by any, came from behind and **touched** the border of His garment. And immediately her flow of blood stopped. And Jesus said, 'Who **touched** Me?' When all denied it, Peter and those with him said, 'Master, the multitudes throng and press You, and You say, "Who **touched** Me?"' But Jesus said, 'Somebody **touched** Me, for I perceived power going out from Me.' Now when the woman saw that she was not hidden, she came trembling; and falling down before Him, she declared to Him in the presence of all the people the reason she had **touched** Him and how she was healed immediately. And He said to her, 'Daughter, be of good cheer; your faith has made you well. Go in peace.' (Lk. 8.43–48)

Here Luke (himself a medical physician) tells us no less than FIVE times that the woman touched Jesus.

As we shall see in a later chapter, for the woman in question, one touch from the King changed everything.

Another example of an individual touching Jesus is in Luke 7:39, where a woman of the streets enters the dinner party of a Pharisee, being held in Jesus' honour. Luke reports that she washed Jesus' feet with her tears and with fragrant oil, causing indignation:

Now when the Pharisee who had invited Him saw this, he spoke to himself, saying, 'This man, if He were a prophet, would know who and what manner of woman this is who is **touching** Him, for she is a sinner.'

Here we see a woman deeply troubled by guilt and shame recognising in Jesus the mercy and compassion of God. We may reasonably suppose that in touching Jesus she found her healing.

Crowds

An early example of a whole mass of people wanting to touch Jesus can be found in Mark 3:10, where the writer reports that Jesus 'healed many, so that as many as had afflictions pressed about Him to **touch** Him'. The same Gospel writer tells us in chapter 6 that 'wherever He entered, into villages, cities, or the country, they laid the sick in the marketplaces, and begged Him that they might just **touch** the hem of His garment. And as many as **touched** Him were made well' (v.56). Here the verb 'touch' is used twice in reference to the crowds of sick people.

Like Mark, Luke makes it clear that one touch from the King changed everything and everyone! In Luke 6:19 he says, 'And the whole multitude sought to **touch** Him, for power went out from Him and healed them all.'

We find the same thing in Matthew 14:34–36:

> When they had crossed over, they came to the land of Gennesaret. And when the men of that place recognized Him, they sent out into all that surrounding region, brought to Him all who were sick, and begged Him that they might only **touch** the hem of His garment. And as many as **touched** it were made perfectly well.

Here the verb 'touch' is used twice. Matthew stresses that the sick were 'completely healed'. Again, just one touch changed everything.

There's No One Like Him

So there are two types of incident in the Synoptic Gospels (i.e. Matthew, Mark and Luke): there are those in which Jesus touches the sick, and those in which the sick touch Jesus. Everyone who is touched by Jesus, or who reaches out to touch him, experiences God's life-transforming power.

Now all this marks Jesus of Nazareth out as utterly unique in two respects.

The first concerns the uniqueness of his ministry two thousand years ago. No one before Jesus had ever healed the sick with just one touch. Theologians like Otto Weinreich used to claim that the early church invented all these Gospel stories of healing by a mere touch. They claimed the church decided to copy Greek myths of gods who healed sick mortals by the power of a touch. The Gospel accounts were accordingly treated as fiction.

More recent research has revealed this to be the very opposite of the case. In an article called 'Healing by a Mere Touch as a Christian Concept', Pieter Lalleman proved conclusively that Otto Weinreich had been completely wrong in his research. There are in fact no cases of such healings before the rise of Christianity. Jesus is unique in this regard. Healings arising from a touch (either the healer touching the sick person, or the sick person touching the healer) appear *for the first time* in the Gospels. There are no precedents in the Greek or Jewish literature before Jesus. The one example that looks remotely parallel concerns the Emperor Hadrian, who lived one hundred years AFTER Jesus! Lalleman concludes that this idea is unique to the Gospels and simply could not have been made up. The idea has to go back to the actual ministry of Jesus, which contained countless examples of one touch from the King changing everything.

So Jesus is unique in respect of his ministry two thousand years ago. And he is secondly unique in respect of his ministry today.

The author of the Letter to the Hebrews in the New Testament says that 'Jesus Christ is the same yesterday, today, and forever' (13:8). Jesus healed the sick yesterday in his earthly ministry. And he still heals the sick today. One touch from the King changed everything for the sick in the first century. And one touch from the King can change everything for the sick in the twenty-first century too. In this respect, there truly is no one quite like Jesus. He still does extraordinary miracles today!

Take the following incident as an example.

In 2005 my prayer partner and close friend J.John visited Cyprus. He went to a place called St Barnabas' monastery. While he was there he was told about an extraordinary miracle that had occurred the week before. A paralysed man had had a dream of the monastery. In the dream he was told he would be healed there. The moment he was taken into the monastery he was totally and instantly healed. He got out of his wheelchair and was 100% restored. The incident attracted national TV coverage on the news.

What was all the more remarkable was the reaction of those present at the monastery. One of them was a Muslim tour guide who got into conversation with J.John. When he asked her if she had witnessed the miracle, she replied that she had seen it. J.John asked her what she made of it. She said, 'I am a Muslim, and I have no framework for understanding miracles in my faith.'

J.John was then able to tell her that he was a Christian and that his faith was in Jesus, who healed the sick in his ministry two thousand years ago, and who still heals the sick today.

Truly, Jesus was unique two thousand years ago in his healing ministry. He is unique today.

There is no one like Jesus!

Jesus is the True King

It is one thing to read about the royal healers of Middle Earth and to speculate about the royal touch of ancient monarchs. It is quite another to read of the healing touch of the King of kings and to experience that same touch in the twenty-first century.

Today we are well aware that touch is critical for a sense of well-being and wholeness. This is true of all human beings from early infancy onwards. A lack of touch or 'tactile deprivation' can have a very destructive impact on physical, emotional and spiritual development, right into adulthood. Many people lack wholeness and freedom because of what is called 'touch hunger'.

The good news is that ever since the dawn of time God has been reaching out to his fallen, wounded children, seeking to touch them with his life-giving love. There is in other words a divine touch that we can all experience – a touch that is neither myth, magic nor manipulation but sheer miracle. This divine touch is the royal touch of the King of kings, Jesus of Nazareth. Thanks to his death on the Cross and his resurrection from the dead, Jesus Christ is alive today. Through the power of the Holy Spirit he is able to minister the King's touch in a way that brings salvation in its fullest and deepest dimensions – that is, forgiveness of sins, the healing of sickness, and deliverance from spiritual oppression.

This book is about the transforming touch of the King of kings. I believe with all my heart that Jesus can touch our lives today. When that happens, miracles invade our world.

And it's really *miracles* on which I want to focus. In my view, there is a difference between healings and miracles. Healings can happen gradually, miracles happen instantly. Healings can involve a process, miracles involve a crisis. Healings can be partial, miracles are total. Healings can involve remissions, miracles involve cures. The Apostle Paul distinguished between healing gifts and the gift of miracles in 1 Corinthians 12:8–10 (NIV):

> To one there is given through the Spirit the message of wisdom, to another the message of knowledge by means of the same Spirit, to another faith by the same Spirit, to another **gifts of healing** by that one Spirit, to another **miraculous powers**, to another prophecy, to another distinguishing between spirits, to another speaking in different kinds of tongues, and to still another the interpretation of tongues.

Not only does Paul distinguish here between the 'gifts of healing' and 'miraculous powers', but also at the end of this same chapter he distinguishes between those who have a ministry in the miraculous and those who have a ministry of healing:

> And in the church God has appointed first of all apostles, second prophets, third teachers, **then workers of miracles, also those having gifts of healing,** those able to help others, those with gifts of administration, and those speaking in different kinds of tongues. (1 Cor. 12:28)

When I talk about 'one touch from the King', I am referring to the gift of miracles – an instant, total, critical transformation.

Don't you long for that kind of manifestation?

God wants us to believe and pray for more of his miraculous, royal touch, especially in the lives of the sick. He wants us to thank him for his healings but press in for his miracles. If you have a holy discontent about the lack of signs and wonders in the contemporary church, then read on. If you feel spiritually impoverished, take heart: the poor in spirit are promised the blessing of God's rule.

My prayer for you is that as you read, you will experience that one touch from the King that changes everything. Elvis was alive, but now is dead. Jesus was dead, but is now alive for evermore. He's the true King. He's the real deal. So seek his touch. It changes everything.

> Let all men know how empty
> and worthless is the power
> of kings. For there is none
> worthy of the name but God,
> whom heaven, earth and sea
> obey.
>
> King Canute

Chapter 2

The King's First Move

In Michelangelo's fresco 'The Creation of Adam', painted on the ceiling of the Sistine Chapel, God stretches out his hand towards Adam. Resting on a bed of grass, Adam stretches out his hand to meet God's touch. With God's and Adam's fingers almost touching, this enduring image calls us to ask, 'What spark of divine life passed between the fingers of God and man?' Michelangelo's majestic painting highlights the great miracle that occurs when God makes contact with our world. It is a powerful picture of the King's touch, a touch that brings life, even to the dead!

A Miracle at Nain

There is a great illustration of this truth in Luke 7, where we see Jesus and his disciples walking the twenty-five miles from Capernaum to Nain. Jesus approaches Nain from the north-east via Endor. He and his followers would have seen the walls and the gates of this once great place as they drew nearer. The name 'Nain' meant 'pleasant', and pleasant it most certainly was, with its lush fruit trees and its opulent gardens.

Roughly ten minutes away from the walls, Jesus and his followers are met by the sight of a band of mourners coming towards the burial ground nearby. It is early evening, the time when funerals take place. In such a culture, the custom would have been for the travellers from Capernaum to stop their journey and show respect for the dead by joining the mourners as they went to bury their loved one. This they do.

Near the head of the procession is a woman. Her torn upper garment – which she has rent in her grief – reveals that she is the mother of the dead boy. She has been weeping for hours and her eyes look bloodshot. The last hours have been spent in preparing her son's body for burial – cutting his hair and nails (as she had done when he was a child) and placing the body in wrappings, known in Hebrew as 'the provision for the journey'. She is absolutely desolate. Not only has she lost her son but she has also already lost her husband. She is a widow without a male in her house. She is economically without hope.

The mother is in that deep mourning which precedes the burial of a loved one. She is led by the funeral orator who proclaims the good deeds of her son, and by sundry Galilean women. Her son's body is carried behind, not in a closed coffin, but on an open bier in wicker wood. The boy's face is uncovered, his eyes closed. His hands are folded on his chest. Various items treasured by him have been placed with him on his last journey. There are holes in the long basket in which poles have been placed. The ends of these are carried by the boy's friends and relatives, who walk barefoot. It is a tragic and desolate scene. The sound of loud lamentation pierces the atmosphere.

But there is hope. The procession for the dead has run into the Prince of Life! Here life and death meet in a collision that will change everything for the widow. Jesus sees her and his heart bleeds for her in her agony. Overflowing with compassion, he says to her, 'Don't cry.' Then he walks past the mother to the wooden bier on which the boy has been carefully placed. There are no great histrionics from Jesus. There are no incantations or loud declarations. Luke (who alone records this great miracle) simply says that Jesus touched the coffin. According to Jewish law he should not have done that. Touching a dead body resulted in the worst kind of defilement. But Jesus does not worry about such matters. The law of love supersedes the love of law and he reaches out his hand.

There is a gasp of amazement as everyone, fixed to the spot, watches what happens next. Jesus, having touched the coffin, merely utters one sentence: 'Young man, I say to you, arise.' Immediately the boy sits up and Luke reports that he begins to speak to those around him, no doubt to his friends who had carried him there. What he said is not recorded, though we can be sure that all were overcome with awe.

In a final touch of divine love, Luke tells us that Jesus gave the boy to his mother. Forgetful of the great crowd of amazed onlookers, Jesus focuses on mother and son and returns the boy to his mother, and in the process restores hope.

While Jesus is forgetful of the crowd, the crowd is not forgetful of Jesus. A great and holy fear wells up within their hearts at this encounter with the numinous, with the divine. Their testimony starts to run like wildfire both locally and across borders. 'This man is a mighty prophet.' And most telling of all, 'We have seen *the hand* of the Lord today.'

And that they had. Two processions had met in a moment of divine and providential synchronicity. One procession represented life, the other death. In that history-making moment, the Author of Life stretched out his hand – the hand of the Lord, no less – and touched a coffin. And that one touch from the King changed everything.

The Royal Initiative

What we learn from this poignant episode is that there were times when Jesus touched people in great need. That touch was not requested by the boy's mother. It was certainly not requested by the boy himself. Nevertheless, Jesus acted and his momentary contact with the coffin was sufficient to cause a miracle that has moved readers for nearly two thousand years. In the midst of death, the touch of the King brought the power of the future age into our world. Heaven invaded earth at the end of the King's hand and something of the climax of history – when the general resurrection will take place – broke into history ahead of time.

Many of the Gospel episodes describing the King's touch reveal Jesus taking the initiative like this. Here we see something of what the Reformers called 'the sovereignty of God', a theme evident everywhere in the Bible. For example, in Psalm 103 verse 19 David says, 'The LORD has established His throne in heaven, and His kingdom rules over all.' David makes a longer declaration of this truth in 1 Chronicles 29:10–12:

> Blessed are You, LORD God of Israel, our Father, forever and ever.
> Yours, O LORD, is the greatness,
> The power and the glory,
> The victory and the majesty;
> For all that is in heaven and in earth is Yours;
> Yours is the kingdom, O LORD,
> And You are exalted as head over all.
> Both riches and honour come from You,
> And You reign over all.
> In Your **hand** is power and might;
> In Your **hand** it is to make great
> And to give strength to all.

The healing ministry of Jesus reveals a lot about the sovereignty of God. Jesus said that he only ever did what he saw the Father doing and that he only ever said what he heard the Father saying. It is for this reason that Jesus reveals God's absolute freedom and total independence in deciding whom he will touch with his supreme power. There were probably other funerals that evening in the region around Galilee besides this one at Nain. But only this boy experiences the King's touch. There were almost certainly other sick and disabled people in the crowds following Jesus and the crowds following the funeral. But only this one boy receives the King's touch – or so we are led to believe. God is sovereign and it is out of his supreme will that he chose to stretch out his hand towards the dead boy from Nain.

God is Sovereign

It is important to accept God's sovereignty if we are to see the King's touch in and through our lives. To put it bluntly: he is 'the King of kings and Lord of lords' (1 Tim. 6:15) – we are not. 'The Lord God Omnipotent reigns' (Rev. 19:6) – we don't!

Not long ago a friend of mine returned from a ministry trip in Russia. He had been the guest of a man called Sergei, head of an organisation called the Exodus Church. Sergei had been a member of the Russian mafia and also a chronic heroin addict. While in prison he was given a Bible, which meant nothing to him at the time. On completing his sentence he went to kill the person who had informed on him. On the way he felt compelled to go into an old church. He stood alone at the front. Suddenly all around him it started to rain gold leaf. Sergei fell to the ground and Jesus revealed himself to him and spoke with him. Immediately the addiction lifted. On the floor of this Rostov church the Exodus Church was born.

Sergei then called together the addicts he knew in the mafia leadership, and as he prayed for them each one had an immediate healing from addiction to drugs. The Exodus church has 45 rehabilitation centres and 45 churches. Already three thousand have been delivered from drugs. President Putin has commended the work, commenting that they are ten times more successful than the state's centres. Exodus has a proven 80% success rate.

Often the recovered addicts go to a city, take a room and invite the addicts from the streets to live with them. Within a year these become churches of 200–300 people, two-thirds of whom are ex-addicts.

My friend concluded, 'I have never known the sheer power of God that I experienced as we travelled and ministered in some of these churches. The congregations were between two hundred and three thousand. It was awesome and I am only now trying to understand it all.'

What an amazing testimony to the sovereignty of God! God is King and he decides whom he will touch. As God says in Exodus 33:19, 'I will be gracious to whom I will be gracious, and I will have compassion on whom I will have compassion.' We shouldn't question this either. Romans 9:20–21 (NIV) says this:

> 'Shall what is formed say to him who formed it, "Why did you make me like this?"' Does not the potter have the right to make out of the same lump of clay some pottery for noble purposes and some for common use?

In other words, God is free in his sovereignty to shape us in whatever way he wills. Sometimes his hands will transform us with healing. Sometimes his hands will mould us through hardships.

The King's Touch Today

Having said that, God's hand is at work today! I have seen the sovereign touch of the King occurring in two major ways. The first is in an immediate way (God working independently). The second is in a mediated way (God working through us).

In the first, God appears to bypass human agency and touch the sick person directly. Let me put it another way: in 'immediate' cases, God stretches out his hand and touches a sick person without any human intermediary being involved.

I remember a few years ago talking to a leading UK surgeon. He was telling me about his daughter, who had been severely injured in a car crash. Over time she recovered somewhat and, after giving her life to Christ in the hospital, came home to her children. However, her future looked bleak medically. Her pelvis had been crushed and had come permanently out of alignment. She would always walk with a limp and at an angle.

One Sunday morning the surgeon and his wife went to take the children to church. They left their daughter with a tape on the healing ministry of Jesus. She listened to it after they had all left. For some reason, the person who taped the talk left the machine running so that it recorded the ministry time as well as the teaching. On the tape the speaker said that he sensed the Holy Spirit saying just two words: 'pelvic realignment'. As he said those words, the woman listening to the tape stood to her feet. 'That's me,' she cried. And as she did so, the power of God came upon her and she began to walk. By the time she was at the other end of the room she was 100% healed.

I was impacted by that not least because the person telling me was someone who had not until then been open to the gifts of the Spirit, including miracles. He was also a leading surgeon who would have wanted scientific proof for everything. On both counts he was predisposed, in my opinion, to scepticism. Yet he was clearly revelling in his daughter's miraculous healing and marvelling at the extraordinarily sovereign way that God had acted. He had truly witnessed the King's touch.

That is what I mean by an 'immediate' touch. There were no human intermediaries in the healing itself. To be sure, people were praying for the daughter, and the father had left a tape about healing with her. But in the final analysis God acted without the laying-on of human hands and touched this daughter's life when she was on her own, and that moment changed everything.

The second way in which we see the sovereignty of God in miracles is through a mediated touch. In these instances God does a sovereign work of healing 'through the hands' of his people. Sometimes this can happen almost 'accidentally', without the human agent being really aware of it.

In the introduction to this book I told the story of a man called Hank. At the end of a meeting where I had spoken he came and shook hands with me. I intended nothing more than to reciprocate the gesture rather reluctantly. But in the process the man was healed and later gave his life to Jesus Christ. That is an example of what I mean by an 'almost accidental' touch.

Another example happened to the celebrated twentieth-century healing evangelist Smith Wigglesworth. His son records an occasion when the great man was waxing eloquent on a stage. He was preaching more and more fervently and in the process he was becoming more and more boisterous. His son was sitting on the front row watching him nervously. He could tell that his father was getting perilously close to the edge of the stage and was in danger of falling off. Sure enough, a few minutes later, the inevitable happened and Smith fell forwards off the stage. He managed to land on his feet and started to career down the centre aisle of the building. There was a man sitting on the front row in desperate need of healing. As Smith ran forwards he reached out his hand to steady himself, momentarily touching the man's shoulder. Smith managed to stabilise himself and the man was instantly, completely healed of his condition!

That again can be defined as an almost accidental touch. There was no premeditation on Smith's part. It just happened. It was a mediated touch, but it was also very much a mysterious, sovereign act of God!

Having said that, this kind of apparently 'accidental' touch is at the moment more exceptional than normal. More often God moves in a sovereign way through the laying-on of hands. Take Gareth's story as an example:

When I was 14 years old, I awoke during the night very hot, out of breath and soaking wet with sweat. I sat up and my breathing was very heavy. I could hear this thumping noise in the back of my head. As I came to, I realised that it was my heart beating that I could hear. I could feel my chest pumping. My heart was beating maybe three or four times a second. I hadn't got a clue what was happening to me. I ran in to my mum and dad's room and shouted, 'My heart, my heart.' As you can imagine, they jumped up terrified. My mum came downstairs with me. My heart just wouldn't stop racing. It was like I had just done some serious exercise. It stopped as quickly as it started.

We went to the doctor's first thing the next morning. I was referred to a cardiac specialist. A few weeks later I went into hospital and had various checks. I had a Computed Axial Tomography scan, was put on an ECG, had blood taken and

every other test imaginable. It was a terrifying experience. I
didn't know God then, but I did say, 'Keep me alive.'

All the tests where done and I was sent home. A few weeks
later I was called back to see a consultant with the results. I was
told I had Wolf Parkinson White Syndrome. They explained to
me I had an extra pathway in my heart which, once stimulated,
causes an abnormal heartbeat. That to me didn't sound good.
They said they would keep an eye on it.

I was fine until one night I had finished my duty as a police
officer and had just got home. I recognised the signs as I lay in
bed. My heart started to go again. It was harder than normal. I
knew I had to act.

I went into hospital and had an ECG. The cardiac specialist
looked at the results. He pointed out clearly where the
abnormality was and referred me to a specialist. He was of the
opinion I might need surgery.

On the day this had happened, I had arranged to catch
up with some of my friends who I had met at Holy Trinity
Church in Brompton about seven years ago. One of them is
head surgeon of a hospital in Hertfordshire. I had talked with
him before about my condition and he had carried out some
research for me. It had never gone any further than that. I was
always scared of what they might find or tell me.

I went to the meeting in London and he was there. I told him
what had happened earlier. He told me that this was serious
and advised that I get help straight away. Before I went home
that night, he prayed for my healing. He placed his hands on
my chest and asked the Lord to heal my heart.

The surgeon who prayed for me contacted me the next day
and gave me a number for a private specialist in London. I
rang it and arranged an appointment. I was told that he was
one of the best cardiologists in the country. The doctor came
to reception and invited me in with my wife Lucy to his
consultation room. I explained my history to him and what
had happened recently. He put an ECG monitor on my chest,
hands and feet to see exactly what my heart was doing. This
took about fifteen minutes. He studied the results and said, 'I
can't see anything wrong with your results. They look perfect.'
I said, 'Are you sure? I have had this condition for years.' He
said, 'You don't have it now.'

I turned to my wife Lucy on the way out of the hospital and
said, 'I have been healed!' I rang my friends and parents right

away and told them the news. I contacted the NHS and spoke to the specialist who had looked at my previous ECG printout. He got it from my file and said it was completely clear. This was the same ECG that I had seen with the specialist who showed me the abnormalities on it. The ECG that said I had been sick now told a completely different story. I received a letter of discharge from the hospital, which said that *by chance* my condition has gone. Having lived and experienced this, chance is not an option.

When the Sick are Not Healed

As we have seen, there are times when God moves with obvious sovereignty, taking the initiative to touch the sick. But, let's face it, there are also times when we pray earnestly for 'just one touch from the King' and we do not get the kind of miracle witnessed in Nain or experienced by Gareth. Why doesn't God answer dramatically in one case when he does in another?

Very recently I had to ask these questions in a way that was acutely painful. A man very dear to me called Phil became seriously ill with cancer. Phil was in his seventies and was a grandfather to my children and a father figure to me. He and his wife Helen have been amazing friends and supporters in my ministry. It is hard to express just how much we love them as a family.

So it was very tough to hear that Phil had cancer. We could see him losing weight and looking more and more gaunt. But we were determined to beat it. Developing a fighting spirit, we prayed fervently for his healing as a church.

I remember visiting Phil shortly before he died. We talked about travelling two tracks simultaneously: the track of prevailing prayer for a miracle, and the track of getting ready for heaven. In the end, we focused almost exclusively on the first and implored God to save and heal him.

Just a week or so after this visit I received a phone call from Helen saying that Phil had just died. It was all so sudden. He was due to have a further visit to the consultant to find out where the cancer was. There were no signs visibly that Phil was close to death. Yet that Monday God took Phil home. I went to the hospital straight away and stood beside his dead body. Helen and I wept. We even took Phil by the hand and prayed for a resurrection touch from the King, but to no avail.

After I had come home, one of my staff team rang me. She had heard about Phil's death and wanted to share something that had happened that morning. Praying for Phil with her husband, she had had a vision of Phil in the sky. His body was lying flat and it was the length of the horizon. She saw the Father with his hands around Phil's head, pulling him heavenward. She saw a number of people at his feet, trying to pull him down to earth. And she sensed God saying, 'Will you please just let him go.'

A few days later I was at a retreat for church leaders. I found myself with the privilege of talking to Dr David Carr, who has been running healing meetings with astonishing results for several years in Solihull in the UK. He has seen many miracles. I asked him how he coped theologically with what I had just been through with Phil. His answer was profound and changed my thinking entirely.

David told me that every time he prays for a person with a serious, life-threatening illness he asks them a simple question: 'Do you sense the Father calling you home?' It doesn't matter what age the person is. That is the question he asks. If they say no, he asks, 'Is the Father telling you to pray for healing?' If they say yes, then he prays with fervour and faith for them to be made well. If they say, 'I don't know,' he still prays for healing.

What really fascinated me was David's description of his response when a person says yes to the question, 'Do you think it's time to go home to the Father?' He told me that he considers there is far too little teaching and celebration about the glory of heaven. We are far too earthbound. And for that reason we tend to regard death as the ultimate tragedy and failure, when for a Christian it is the gateway to being with the Lord Jesus. If a person responds that they feel it's time to die, we should release them with joy. To live is Christ but to die is gain! Let them go to be with the Lord. This isn't defeat, it's victory! We shouldn't fight for their healing if they are being called to go home to heaven.

He then told me the story of a man he had prayed for who was very seriously ill. He went to see him. He asked the man whether he thought God was calling him home and the man said yes. David then asked if he had put his house in order and was ready now. With his wife present, he said yes. David then took the man's head in his arms and placed it on his shoulder. He said this to the man: 'Then I release you now in the name of Jesus. Give my love to him when you see him.' And with that the man died immediately and peacefully.

David then talked to me about letting go. He told me that there are many times when God calls us to pray for healing miracles. But there are also times when he calls us to release Christians so that they can 'die well'. Dying well was an idea that intrigued me, so I asked David about that. He said that he didn't believe it was God's will for us to spend months and months with tubes sticking in and out of every part of our body, waiting to die in great discomfort. He felt that it is the Father's will that we die what he called 'a dignified death'. Letting people go, when God wills it, is as important as praying for healing. The critical thing in it all is, 'What does the Father want?'

And here we come back again to the sovereignty of God. He is King of kings, we are not. He reigns over all, we don't. What I learned in Phil's case changed me. I should have asked him what the Father was saying and I should have really asked myself that question. But I simply didn't want to confront reality because, as the poet said, human beings cannot bear very much reality. As I came to God in repentance, I felt the Holy Spirit say something to my heart that I now live by. He said, 'Don't pull people back into infirmity when you are called to release them into infinity.'

God's *Kairos* Moments

When it comes to the King's touch, God is sovereign. That is the abiding lesson I have learned. There are times when God intervenes and one touch from the King changes everything. There are other times when God does not obviously intervene and a person must continue with their sickness, believing for the breakthrough, which may or may not come later on. There are also times when God says, 'It's time to come home,' and in that situation, heaven is that person's healing.

The key word in what I have just said is the word 'time'. The Bible contains a great deal of revelation about time. One thing that becomes very clear from any reading of Scripture is that God's timescale is different from ours. He has a very different view of time from ours. Our earthbound view means that we are severely limited, seeing things only from a partial rather than a panoramic perspective, from a transient rather than an eternal viewpoint.

There are times in the Gospels when Jesus highlights the difference between the divine and human understandings of time. One of the best examples is with Lazarus in John chapter 11. Here Lazarus' sisters send a message to Jesus that their brother is sick. He delays three days before answering and when he arrives Lazarus is dead. The sisters both quite understandably tell Jesus, 'If you had been here, my brother would not have died.' However, even though Jesus has arrived apparently too late, a great miracle occurs and Lazarus is raised from death. Healing comes, but it comes later than anticipated or requested.

On another occasion, the brothers of Jesus are trying to persuade him to go up to Jerusalem to celebrate the Feast of Tabernacles and to show his disciples there the works (i.e. the miracles) that he has been doing. Jesus answers in John 7:6 by talking about time:

> Then Jesus said to them, 'My time has not yet come, but your time is always ready.'

Here Jesus is referring to the hour of his glorification in Jerusalem. He is saying that for the disciples, any time will do. But for him, there is a God-ordained timing to the events of his crucifixion, resurrection and return to the Father. Literally, he says, 'You are ready any time; I am not.'

The issue here is therefore one of timing. Jesus uses the Greek word *kairos* in John 7 when he talks about time. *Kairos* refers to a moment in time that is unique and unrepeatable. It is to be distinguished from *chronos*, the word from which we get chronology. *Chronos* refers to ordinary, everyday time. *Kairos* refers to exceptional, divinely ordained moments.

Jesus' point to his brothers is that they live in *chronos* time and that any moment within ordinary time seems right to them when it comes to God acting. He points out that this is wrong. While any time will do for them, only the right time will do for him.

In verse 10 of John 7 we learn that Jesus did respond to his brothers. While his brothers went up to the Feast of Tabernacles at the beginning, Jesus went later on in the feast, and in secret! So Jesus acted, but he acted later than anticipated.

Julie's Story

Julie Sheldon, author of *Dancer Off Her Feet*, tells the story of her miraculous healing. Her testimony points to the mystery of God's *kairos* moments.

> I had been suffering for almost four years with a serious neurological illness called dystonia. I had contracted a 'severe generalised dystonia' which meant most muscles in my body became affected. My right leg was gradually drawn up across my body with my foot inverted. My arms were bent at right angles with my hands in fists with the wrists bent over. Severe muscle spasms pulled my head right over my left hand shoulder and I dribbled and shook. I was unable to feed myself and needed to be dressed and bathed, just as my own two children needed to be helped.
>
> Having trained for fifteen years as a professional ballet dancer, to contract such a hideous looking illness was very humiliating.

I'd been trained and schooled to be in total control of my muscles, producing beautiful lyrical movements, and here I was now being stared at because of the contortions my body was wrapping itself into.

At the height of the illness I needed to be fed by a nasal gastric tube as my swallowing muscles went into spasm, and even found my sight was affected. It was particularly distressing when the excruciating spasms went into 'reverse' and my head would be violently jerked backwards, arms pulled behind my body and legs all tangled up fighting for relief.

Many people over the years had come to visit and pray. Many had left. Sometimes there was a great sense of God's peace after these faithful prayers, but no physical changes seemed to happen, in fact I became worse and worse.

It came to a point when I was in intensive care and friends were coming to say 'goodbye' – thankfully I didn't know this at the time! My older brother even flew in from America with the intention of putting some of his Royal Marine Commando training into practice. He felt it would be kinder to put a pillow over me to 'put me out of my misery' – again I'm thankful not to have known this piece of information!

I knew I was one step away from being put on a ventilator as my breathing was becoming increasingly laboured and difficult with all the spasms and I spent a great deal of time heavily sedated.

It was in this state that a friend called Virginia came to visit. She brought a man with her who I hadn't met before, nor did I really care as I was trying so hard just to take the next breath. Virginia explained that he was called Canon Jim Glennon and he was over from Australia. He very much wanted to pray for my healing and would 'believe' for me.

I've always felt it extremely important to give as accurate an account as I can possibly remember as to what happened that day. I have never wanted to exaggerate or embellish or in any way detract from God's hand on me during that visit, so being mindful of accuracy and given that I was very sedated I give my best narrative to this event.

I remember Jim Glennon asking if he might pray for me and saying that 'he would take it on to believe for me. I didn't have to do anything – he would believe without doubting in his heart that I would be healed'.

His prayer was very simple: 'Thank you, Father, that you are healing me now. Thank you, Jesus, that you are healing me now. Thank you, Holy Spirit, that you are healing me now.'

When he had finished he took a piece of paper and wrote in big capital letters, so I could see them, these words: 'Even when we are too weak to have any faith left, God remains faithful to us and will help us.'

He stuck the paper on the side of my hospital locker in my line of vision and I remember feeling this was very important. I certainly felt far too weak to have any faith left, all I was concentrating on was the next breath, but here was a word of hope. God would remain faithful to me and would help me.

I don't even remember Virginia and Jim Glennon leaving. I fell into a very deep sleep and when I awoke I just felt able to sit up in bed unaided. It had always taken two people to sit me up before, but now I simply was able to do it by myself.

The following day I felt able to get out of bed. My right leg was still in spasm and bent up across my body, but I felt able to walk to the window of the ward on my crutches. I hadn't been out of bed or the wheelchair for a very long time. Very rapidly all the muscle spasms released and bit by bit my body returned to normal – over a very short space of time.

The Professor of Neurology, whose care I was under, was himself astounded at the rapid improvement and although didn't profess to have any faith, was gracious enough to say, 'Something has happened. You have made a miraculous recovery.' From his scientific and medical standpoint he pointed out that 'severe generalised dystonia does not usually remit in this way'.

With my body returning to normal, all drugs were reduced, and I suddenly found myself to be an able-bodied person once again. The most exciting and poignant part was being able to be a mother to our children. Because of the positioning of my leg and disabled arms I could not hold the children on my knee, but all that changed and it was a great moment of joy and healing for all of us.

Another important part of my story starts many years before when I was a ballet dancer. I had been rehearsing with my boy partner and whilst lifting me up his hands slipped and I fell to the floor fracturing my spine. Effectively my career as a ballerina was ended at that moment as I spent six months in a plaster jacket and the same time again recovering. The back injury along with a skiing accident and meningitis may have contributed to me contracting dystonia.

After the incredible healing from this illness I suddenly became very depressed. It felt so 'unfair' to have come through so much only to be plunged into the black hole of depression. A friend came to pray with me and again, like with Jim Glennon, she prayed very simply that God would remove this depression. As she prayed I had a picture of that rehearsal many years previously, and God spoke deep into my spirit. It was if he was saying: 'Julie, I've given you your perfect ballerina body back, but what really needs healing is your heart. You need to forgive. You need to forgive that boy who dropped you during the rehearsal.' It was so vivid and without doubt, God. I hadn't even thought of the boy for years and wasn't really aware that I held a deep grudge against him for ruining my career. I prayed for forgiveness and a release of all I had harboured against him. Immediately the depression lifted.

I offer this as a true testimony. I don't write from a place of triumph as a few years later our younger daughter developed a malignant brain tumour and I've faced questions such as 'Why should you be healed and then your daughter get cancer?' I don't know; I don't understand. But I still trust God, I still pray and I still believe that he is Almighty in our fallen world, and I thank him from the bottom of my heart for his grace and mercy.

Times and Seasons

Julie's testimony is encouraging and at the same time honest. In her account of her miracle, she highlights one of the issues we have been addressing in this chapter, that of timing. Why is it that Julie was prayed for so often by her loved ones without being healed, and then one day a stranger passes through and lays hands on her and she is changed so dramatically?

Julie doesn't avoid this tough question, or the other ones contained in her testimony. In correspondence with me she reported the following:

> One of our young daughters said, 'It's so unfair, Mummy. We prayed for you every night and that man only prayed for you

once and you got better.' Perhaps out of the mouth of babes. But it did appear extraordinary.

When it comes to the King's touch, God is sovereign. He is in complete control of the times and the seasons of our lives. As we read in Ecclesiastes 3:1–2:

> To everything there is a season,
> A time for every purpose under heaven:
> A time to be born,
> And a time to die.

God ordains the times and seasons. In verse 3 we read that there is 'a time to heal'.

There is a moment in God's purposes when miracles occur and someone is touched in such a way that their lives are dramatically and very quickly restored. These times are *kairos* moments, when God does something that causes his name to be glorified and his Kingdom to be expanded. When these occur there is a kind of divine and human synchronicity. It seems as though God's timing and our time-frame coincide with each other to produce a remarkable and history-making event in our own lives and the lives of others.

There truly are moments to be seized in God, moments when God's ready, you're ready and other people are ready. When the tipping point comes, we all need to be ready. When the King makes his move, his timing is perfect. He is never early. He is never late. He is always perfectly on time.

In the end, God's will is the critical factor. As Pastor Barbara Garlington puts it, 'I always teach that healing is up to God. It is about God's will. That way, when the sick are healed, God gets the glory. When they are not healed, I don't get the blame!'

Laying hold upon God is
not the act of a dead man,
neither is it the deed of one
who is destitute of spiritual
perception; it is the act of one
who is quickened and kept
alive by the indwelling power
of the Holy Spirit.

Charles Spurgeon

Chapter 3

Grabbing Hold of God

I noticed it because I love soccer and I am always on the lookout for testimonies of healing. It was all over our very secular British newspapers at the end of the 2005 season. The story concerned a soccer player called Marvin Andrews who played for Glasgow Rangers, one of the most successful Scottish teams in recent decades. The reports in the newspapers ran the headline, 'The Miracle of Marvin Andrews' Knee'. That caught my attention.

Marvin Andrews scored the winning goal on the last day of the season to secure not just victory on the day but the title for the whole season. At the end of the match he knelt down in the centre circle of the pitch to pray and give thanks to the Lord. On his T-shirt the crowd could read words from Luke's Gospel, 'The things that are impossible with me are possible with God.'

Why did Marvin make such a gesture? In a match against Dundee a month before, Andrews had ruptured his anterior cruciate ligament – a 35mm link at the knee between the femur and tibia that provides stability and balance. This is an injury that can end a player's career. The Rangers medical staff told Marvin that he would need surgery followed by months of rehabilitation. But he refused to have the operation and chose instead to go to God in prayer. 'I prayed to God,' he said, 'and he spoke. God is not deaf. He speaks. Some people cannot believe it; they think he doesn't reply. But my God is not like that. When I speak to him he replies. God told me not to have the operation.'

Needless to say, those advising Marvin were appalled. The medical staff told him that he had to have the operation or his career would be over. Marvin comments, 'Doubts came, fear came, the devil tried to bring fear into me, just as the Bible said. There were all different kinds of people speaking negatively, speaking fear into me, but I kept holding on to God. This is what faith is about. God kept telling me, "Keep believing, keep trusting." And that gave me strength.'

Against all odds, within three weeks Marvin Andrews was back playing football. He played the last four games of the season and helped Rangers win the title. His manager Alex McLeish stated, 'Marvin is defying logic.' Marvin himself said this – and this was reported in the national newspapers of Great Britain:

> I'm a servant of the Lord. I'm here to tell people that he is still alive, that we still have the same God that opened the blind eyes and allowed the crippled man to walk. I'm here to continue proclaiming the gospel, to tell people the good news.

The Importance of Faith

In the last chapter we looked at Gospel episodes where Jesus takes the initiative and touches the lives of the sick, bringing miraculous healing. We talked about the sovereignty of God – about God's absolute freedom and supreme power in touching whomsoever he decides to touch. We looked at examples of this royal initiative today – ways in which God has stretched out his hand and healed sick people in the most extraordinary ways. Sometimes this happens immediately – without human intermediary; sometimes it happens in a mediated way, with a believer administering the touch that changes everything.

All this emphasis on God's sovereign touch is good news. At the same time it can become bad news if we're not careful. It can give us cause to become passive. In other words, people who over-emphasise the doctrine of the sovereignty of God can very easily slip into a resignation which looks like determinism. 'Well, God is sovereign. If he is going to heal me, he'll do it without any help from me.' This almost feels like a 'Que sera, sera' mentality – 'Whatever will be, will be.' Now of course we have to be wise here. God is indeed sovereign and, as we saw in the last chapter, he is perfectly capable of making his move independently of us. All this has ample biblical precedent in those stories where Jesus touches those who are not actively involved in their healing. The best example is the one we studied in Chapter 2, the raising of the widow's boy at Nain. The boy was dead and of course played no part at all in his miracle. He was 100% passive in the process.

At the same time we mustn't stop there. There are not just stories in the Gospels where Jesus touches those in need. There are also episodes where sick people play an active and almost aggressive part in touching Jesus. In these incidents, people who are absolutely desperate pursue the person of Jesus with a deep and unbridled sense of abandonment. In these situations it seems almost as if it is their faith that secures the healing. In these instances, grabbing hold of Jesus seems to be the critical factor in determining the outcome they desired. They run hard after the King in order to reach out and touch him, and as they do so, it changes everything in their world.

All this highlights the human part played in miracles. Miracles are always the result of God's will, yes. But they also occur in environments where someone has real faith. The reason why I like Marvin Andrews' testimony is because it is the testimony of a man who believed that nothing is impossible for God, who grabbed hold of God's promises and continued to exercise faith even when others were speaking negatively to him. That is not passivity! That is not a deterministic 'Whatever will be, will be.' That is faith.

The Woman who Touched the King

You may have anticipated the incident I am going to describe now. Mark talks about it in chapter 5 of his Gospel, Matthew in chapter 9 and Luke in chapter 8. Jesus is on his way to the house of a synagogue ruler called Jairus, whose 12-year-old daughter is very sick. The dad manages to get Jesus to come to his house. On the way Jesus is delayed by the conduct of a woman desperate for healing. Luke records the incident as follows:

> Now a woman, having a flow of blood for twelve years, who had spent all her livelihood on physicians and could not be healed by any, came from behind and touched the border of His garment. And immediately her flow of blood stopped. And Jesus said, 'Who touched Me?' When all denied it, Peter and those with him said, 'Master, the multitudes throng and press You, and You say, "Who touched Me?"' But Jesus said, 'Somebody touched Me, for I perceived power going out from Me.' Now when the woman saw that she was not hidden, she came trembling; and falling down before Him, she declared to Him in the presence of all the people the reason she had touched Him and how she was healed immediately. And He said to her, 'Daughter, be of good cheer; your faith has made you well. Go in peace.' (Lk. 8:43–48)

There are many things that are important to notice about this incident. I'd like to point to five in particular.

First, note the way in which Luke emphasises the power of just one touch in this episode. Five times he uses the verb *haptomai*, to touch, in the report of this incident. Luke was a physician. As a medic he seems fascinated by the healing effects of touching the King. All the woman did was touch Jesus, and this changed absolutely everything. This fact alone clearly intrigues Dr Luke.

The second thing we should note is that the woman was 'unclean'. Her bleeding disorder made her impure in the eyes of the Rabbis. Yet Jesus does not condemn her for touching him, nor does he believe himself unclean. Jesus touches the 'untouchables', and the 'untouchables' touch Jesus. Indeed, he goes on to Jairus' house to touch the girl who is now dead.

That brings me thirdly to the mention of 'twelve years'. The girl was 12 years old. The woman had had the bleeding disorder for twelve years. This means that the girl was born in the year that the woman began to suffer from her infirmity. This sounds like another example of 'Kingdom synchronicity'. These two lives – joined by the number of years mentioned – are wonderfully transformed on the very same day.

The fourth thing to note is the way that Jesus stops a whole crowd for just one person. There was a sense of urgency, at least in Jairus. He wanted to get Jesus to his daughter as soon as he possibly could. But when the woman touched Jesus, he stopped the entire procession in order to find out who it was. That speaks to me of the profound compassion of Jesus. He did not live by the tyranny of the urgent. He lived a life of love.

The final thing I want to mention is the woman's faith. She had spent all her money on consulting medics and they had not managed to cure her problem. It would have been possible for her at this point to say, 'I am going to have to live with this. It must be God's will.' But she does not. Hearing that Jesus is in town, she pursues him through the crowd, desperate to touch the garment of the King. Why does she do that? What is going on in her heart? The only thing we can say is that she must have heard the testimonies of Jesus' healing miracles and that faith – which comes by hearing – has welled up in her heart.

Faith means 'believing what you cannot see'. Or, as St Augustine said, 'Faith is to believe what we do not see; the reward of faith is to see what we believe.' The woman cannot see her healing. Yet she believes that she is going to receive it. So she presses in and grabs hold of the Royal Healer and in doing so she is *immediately* healed. Jesus' words conclude the story: 'Your faith has made you well.' Matthew Henry puts it very compassionately:

> Her faith was very strong; for she doubted not but that by the touch of the hem of his garment she should derive from him healing virtue sufficient for her relief, looking upon him to be such a full fountain of mercies that she should steal a cure and he not miss it. Thus many a poor soul is healed, and helped, and saved, by Christ, that is lost in a crowd, and that nobody takes notice of.

However hard we try, we cannot escape the importance of faith in this passage. Like Marvin Andrews, the woman in Luke 8 has heard many unpromising things from the medics in her life and yet she chooses to believe that Jesus has the power to heal her. That implies at least some human part in the healing event. Some of course will argue that faith is a divine gift and that her belief in Jesus' power was inspired by God. Even if that's true in this case, the woman still had to co-operate with God. She was not a robot programmed to believe. She was not compelled to run hard after the Healer. She chose to be active in the process. She made the decision to put her trust in Jesus and to believe that nothing is too hard for the Lord. In a time of extreme trouble, she pushed past all her doubts and fears and broke into the presence of her Deliverer. No wonder Jesus applauded her faith.

The Hem of Jesus' Garment

But what was her faith in, exactly? To answer that question we need to understand the Jewish background to the story. In particular, we need to understand why it is that the woman touches 'the hem of Jesus' garment'. What did Luke mean by this phrase?

In Jesus' day, Jewish men wore a woollen outer garment called the *tallit*. On each of the four corners of this garment there were tassels known as *tzitzit*. These *tzitzit* were extremely important for religious reasons. They were worn in accordance with Numbers 15:37–40, where the Lord tells Moses to instruct his people to make tassels to wear on their garments for all future generations. These tassels were to be a reminder of all the commandments of the Lord, a stimulus to obey all that God required to live a holy life.

According to Jewish expert Dwight Pryor, the *tzitzit* had a specific design. Each tassel consisted of eight strands of thread. Four strands (three white and one blue) were looped through an opening in the corner of the garment and then folded over to become eight in total. These eight strands were then tied in a series of five double knots.

All of this was extremely important in terms of symbolism. The five knots were a reminder of the Torah, which consisted of the first five books of the Bible. The four strands were a reminder of the Tetragrammaton, the four Greek letters that made up the sacred covenant name for God revealed to Moses (YHWH). The number 13 (8+5) was a reminder of the oneness of God. The word *echad* in Hebrew has the numeric value of 13, and this word means 'one', as in 'the Lord is one' (i.e. indivisible). The word *tzitzit* itself has a numerical value of 600, which when added to the 13 already stated above makes 613. In Jewish tradition there were 613 commandments in the five books of the Torah.

The tassels on Jesus' outer garment were therefore extremely rich in terms of their symbolism. They stood for the sacred name of God (the four strands), the instructions of God (the five double knots), the oneness of God (the eight strands tied in five double knots) and the totality of God's commandments (600+13).

According to a Jewish interpretation of this passage, the woman was expressing faith in God in the fullest sense. She was not directing her faith towards some supposed mystical properties in the tassels themselves. That would have been superstition. Rather, she was reaching out to the wholeness of who God is, and in the process she experienced wholeness! As Dwight Pryor puts it, she was effectively saying, 'If I can but lay hold of the totality or the fullness of God: who he is; his nature, his word and his will – i.e., if I can but touch the wholeness of God – I myself can be made whole' (www. jcstudies.com). Now that's what I call 'faith'.

The Kingdom is for the Desperate

One of my great heroes is George Muller, who built orphanages in Bristol during the nineteenth century. He lived entirely by faith and said this: 'Faith does not operate in the realm of the possible. There is no glory for God in that which is humanly possible. Faith begins where man's power ends.'

This kind of faith is often vital for receiving the touch of the King that changes everything. A holy desperation is required if we are to persevere and see the breakthroughs we long for. Passive faith (which is really a contradiction in terms) will not do. Scepticism is not helpful. What is needed is active, living, dynamic faith that springs from a passionate pursuit of God.

The great revival theologian Jonathan Edwards had a great name for this kind of thing. He called it 'pressing into the Kingdom of God'. In a sermon with that same title Edwards once defined what he meant:

> Pressing into the kingdom of heaven denotes earnestness and firmness of resolution. There should be strength of resolution, accompanying strength of desire, as it was in the psalmist: 'one thing have I desired, and that will I seek after.'

Edwards went on to say:

> There are two things needful in a person, in order to possess these strong resolutions; there must be a sense of the great importance and necessity of the mercy sought, and there must also be a sense of opportunity to obtain it, or the encouragement there is to seek it.

While Edwards did not believe that divine healing was available in his own day, his principles are still relevant. The woman in Luke 8 was certainly earnest and firm in her resolution. Furthermore, the woman had both necessity and opportunity. She desperately needed healing and she saw in Jesus the opportunity of her healing. The Kingdom of God is truly for the desperate.

Helen's Story

Not long ago we invited Bishop Joseph and Pastor Barbara Garlington over to our church, St Andrew's Chorleywood. They minister in Pittsburgh in a wonderful growing and vibrant church. They brought their choir over with them and we had an extraordinary weekend in the presence of God together, worshipping, listening to great teaching and going to the next level in our walk with God.

One of the many people in our church transformed by this visit was a young woman called Helen, a theology graduate who had experienced major illness and disability in her time at university. Desperate for healing, she pressed through the crowds in our church on the Sunday morning to ask Pastor Barbara (who heads up the healing ministry at their church in Pittsburgh) to pray for her. Helen tells the story in her own words:

> When I was 21, in my final year of university, I had to have spine surgery and during my recovery I found out that I was partially deaf in both ears. This knocked me for six as I had just had eight months of real hardship, and then to find this out really tested my faith and dependency on God.
>
> I was very tired of dealing with things so just accepted it. When Mark Stibbe gave a talk on being desperate for God's healing touch, I had no idea how to be desperate. The exhaustion and emotional numbness far exceeded my ability to seek healing actively. It was as if I was resigned to the fact that I had this disability. I had to wear a hearing aid for eighteen months – which I hated; it was only in one ear so my hearing still wasn't good and it was very frustrating for me and everyone around me.
>
> Then my tinnitus (which I have had for as long as I can remember) got worse and was constant rather than being intermittent. It was stopping me from sleeping, from concentrating at work, from relaxing; it gave me headaches and I was getting exhausted and full of resentment.
>
> Then came the church weekend when Bishop Joseph and Pastor Barbara Garlington came to our church at St Andrew's. I went to the Friday evening service when the choir from Pittsburgh were singing and just broke down. The exhaustion, the frustration, the headaches had all got too much for me and I just cried. This for me is rather unusual, as I am not a particularly emotional person – especially in public – but I just didn't care, I had had too much.
>
> On the Saturday night I said to God, 'If you want me to go to church on Sunday morning then you had better wake me up.' At

10:30am I woke up and decided that it was not enough time to get ready and stayed in bed. My mum came home from the 9:00 service and challenged me about going, so I went, and Bishop Joseph was talking about being expectant for God's favour. I got really into this and was waiting for the prayer ministry at the end, but there wasn't any. I just couldn't believe it. I am no good at going up for prayer and the one day that I actually wanted to, there wasn't any.

However, I saw Pastor Barbara and I wanted her to pray for me, so I fought the typically British attitude of reserve and found myself walking over to her, not tentatively, but as though nothing was going to prevent me from knocking on God's door about this. I was that desperate. I asked her if she was in a hurry and she said no, so I outlined why I was here and how cross I was that there was no ministry. So she prayed for me and for the first time in a long time the Holy Spirit moved visibly and powerfully on my life. With me he is normally gentle, but not this time. We were waging war together. My attitude towards it was, 'Well, God, I have nothing left, I cannot cope any more; you have to move now.' I am never this assertive but it just didn't seem like there was any option other than God healing me. And he did!

When I relayed this story to my mother she was astounded at me, not because God had healed me, but because I had stepped that far out of character. My desperation led me to obedience and the expectation that God would move. But the flipside of it was that I was fully ready to accept the healing – no doubts, no nonsense – and I think that is why my hearing got better and better the more people I told. The more people I told, the clearer my hearing got, and now I don't use my hearing aid and have very little problem hearing people. I praise God for what He has done.

What is Faith?

Helen showed great faith in that story. But what, then, is faith? This is a question asked by the writer of the Letter to the Hebrews. He begins chapter 11 with these words, 'What is faith? It is the confident assurance that what we hope for is going to happen. It is the evidence of things we cannot yet see' (NLT). How do we come to have such faith?

There are two views here. The first says that this kind of faith is a gift. The thinking behind this is that there are three types of faith talked about in the New Testament. There is first of all what I call 'conversion' faith. This is the faith I had back in 1977 when I confessed my sins and declared that I believed that Jesus is my Saviour, Lord and Friend. On that day way back in 1977 I was justified by faith. I was made right with God by believing in what Jesus Christ has accomplished at the Cross. That is what I mean by 'conversion' faith. You can't become a Christian without it.

But then there is a second kind of faith talked about in the New Testament. I call this 'continuing' faith. When I became a Christian I chose to believe in Jesus. But that was not the end of the matter as regards faith. I have to go on believing in Jesus every day. I need continuing faith, not just conversion faith.

Then thirdly there is what I call 'charismatic' faith. If you remember the list of the spiritual gifts in 1 Corinthians 12 (which I quoted in Chapter 1), you will notice that Paul mentions faith as a charismatic or grace gift in verses 8–11. He qualifies what this kind of faith is at the start of 1 Corinthians 13 when he describes a faith 'that can move mountains'. Charismatic faith is mountain-moving faith. It is a sudden, supernatural surge of confidence that God is going to do something miraculous. It might be the conversion of someone whom we thought would never come to Christ. It might be the healing of someone whom we thought was beyond help. It might be the rescue of a marriage that we considered irreparable. God gives 'charismatic' faith to certain individuals in his church when he is about to move a mountain of impossibility.

A few moments ago I asked the question, 'How do we come to have the kind of faith that constitutes "confident assurance that what we hope for is going to happen"?' The first answer to this question is that we need to pray for the spiritual gift of faith. When it comes to the miraculous and life-changing touch of the King, charismatic (rather than merely continuing) faith is required and this is a gift to be received, not a feeling you can just whip up.

The second answer to the question is that this kind of special faith is something we exercise according to our own choice and initiative. In this way of thinking, faith is something we decide and discipline ourselves to develop over time. It is 'continuing' faith exercised at a higher level. The passage often used to support this view is Mark 4:26–29:

> And He said, 'The kingdom of God is as if a man should scatter seed on the ground, and should sleep by night and rise by day, and the seed should sprout and grow, he himself does not know how. For the earth yields crops by itself: first the blade, then the head, after that the full grain in the head. But when the grain ripens, immediately he puts in the sickle, because the harvest has come.'

Those who believe that special or dynamic faith is something we can all exercise point to the growth of the seed here: first the blade, then the head, then the full grain in the head. They liken faith to the seed. It is supposed to develop, strengthen and grow. To put it another way, faith is like a muscle. It is something we exercise and the more we exercise it the stronger it becomes.

So there are two views that I routinely come across when it comes to faith (understood as the confident assurance that a thing hoped for is going to occur). The first says that this kind of faith is a gift supernaturally and suddenly bestowed by God. The second says that it is something we choose to exercise in a given situation of need and challenge.

A Fighting Faith

The argument over which of these two views is correct will no doubt continue. In the end, however, one thing is certain, that it is impossible to please God without faith (Heb. 11:6). All Christians are called to exercise faith. All Christians are called on a daily basis to believe in what they cannot yet see – to put their trust in invisible Kingdom realities. More than that, the majority of great breakthroughs in the Christian life occur when someone somewhere has exercised what I call 'fighting faith'. Like Helen in the testimony above, they have pursued God with desperation. They have been aggressive, active and determined in their exercise of faith. Helen's story shows that breakthroughs come when a fighting faith has been displayed. As Ralph Erskine says, 'Faith, without trouble or fighting, is a suspicious faith; for true faith is a fighting, wrestling faith.'

In County Armagh in Northern Ireland, a woman called Sharyn Mackay was diagnosed with cancer and told that she had twelve months to live. This mother of four was informed that she had a rare form of cancer that had spread to her lungs and her kidneys. She was told that it was certain she was going to die. Sharyn was devastated by the news. Only the day before, she had celebrated the birthday of one of her children. Now she was being told that she wouldn't live to see the next one.

Sharyn knew that only her Christian faith could help her now. This was all that was left. At this point she heard about some healing meetings that were going on in the Solihull Renewal Centre in England. These meetings were being hosted by Dr David Carr, the pastor I mentioned in the last chapter. Sharyn and her husband William decided they would go. This is how she describes what happened:

> As soon as we entered the building we felt an enormous heat. It was as though there was an incredible presence in the room and an overwhelming feeling of love. As soon as the meeting finished I felt as though the cancer had left my body.

On Friday 8 July 2004 Sharyn and William set off for their hospital to get the latest results. They prayed all the way there, and though naturally very anxious they felt a supernatural peace. When the consultant came in he was smiling. He said, 'Sharyn, you are going to leave the hospital happier than when you came in.' He told Sharyn that she wasn't going to die because every trace of cancer had completely disappeared. Four radiographers had pored over her test results and were astonished to find no cancer in Sharyn's lungs or kidneys. They had no explanation for it.

The couple were overjoyed at this news. Since then they have started their own healing ministry and now encourage other people to believe in the power of prayer. More than that, Sharyn's miraculous recovery has become well known in Northern Ireland, where it is now being taught as part of the curriculum in schools as an example of a modern-day miracle!

What an example of 'fighting faith'. Fighting faith is not faith without anxiety or tears. Fighting faith is a faith that pushes through walls of doubt and fear to a place of breakthrough. Fighting faith is what Sharyn exhibited. Fighting faith is what we see in Helen's story. If you ask me whether this kind of faith is divine or human I would have to say it's both! It's a gift from God, something donated by our loving Heavenly Father. But it is also something that we have to act upon courageously and intentionally. Faith – particularly fighting faith – is a vital ingredient in the King's touch. Fighting faith seizes hold of Jesus when opportunity knocks.

When the King Passes By

Someone once said that the opportunity of a lifetime must be seized in the lifetime of the opportunity. There are moments in the Gospels when the King of kings is passing by and people seize the moment. Not only do they seize the moment, they grab hold of the King. It is as if something deep within their hearts knows that just one touch from this King will change everything.

I wonder whether you have ever been in a situation where you had a once in a lifetime opportunity to shake the hand of someone really famous, someone really influential, someone you respected for their position in life. That happened to my friend J. John and me recently. We were in Washington DC and had the opportunity of going not just to the White House on a tour but into the West Wing for lunch with several Christians who work for the President. We had a great time. Deep down, however, we were both very keen to bump into the President. We wanted to shake hands with him, not because we are closet Republicans but because we knew he was a man of faith and because we knew it would give us a great story!

Well, we didn't see the President during the tour of the West Wing or during lunch in the West Wing Mess. After our meal we left the table and both of us went to the rest room. Once inside we realised we were the only people there. We had seen all the secret agents dressed in black suits and talking into concealed microphones, so we decided to have some fun. We pretended to be secret agents ourselves, talking into our sleeves as we washed and dried our hands. We had a great laugh at the expense of these gentlemen, not realising that they were probably watching us on hidden cameras and having a laugh at our expense too!

As a result of all this childish humour we were longer than we should have been. When we came out the two men who had been escorting us round the West Wing looked at us in despair. They knew how keen we had been to shake hands with the President. Well, while we were wasting time pretending to be secret servicemen the President and the Vice-President had walked past on the way to the situation room. They had stopped to shake the hands of the two gentlemen looking after us. If we had not been play-acting, we too would have been there and would have been able to shake hands with the most powerful man on the planet!

Ever since that moment I have used that story – at my own expense – to encourage people not to waste their opportunity to reach out for the hand of the King. The trouble is there are too many Christians messing around in the rest room when the King of kings is passing by.

A *Diasozo* Move of God

In the Gospels, we see individuals grabbing hold of their opportunity when Jesus passes by. Desperate for just one touch, they reach out to him and find their healing. They don't mess around. They don't waste time. They seize the opportunity of a lifetime in the lifetime of that opportunity.

This happens in the case of individuals, such as the woman with the bleeding disorder. This also happens with whole crowds of people. In fact, one of my favourite examples of this is right at the end of Matthew 14. The disciples have just crossed the lake and arrive at Gennesaret with Jesus. Matthew records that:

> When they had crossed over, they came to the land of Gennesaret. And when the men of that place recognized Him, they sent out into all that surrounding region, brought to Him all who were sick, and begged Him that they might only touch the hem of His garment. And as many as touched it were made perfectly well. (Mt. 14:34–36)

Twice Matthew uses the verb *haptomai*, to touch, in this report. Here we have not just individuals touching Jesus. We have a large number of people touching him.

What characterised all of these people in their desire to touch Jesus? The answer is simple: it was fighting faith. These people really believed that Jesus could change their situation. They believed that if they could get close enough to him, if they could just touch him, then blind eyes would see, deaf ears would hear, lame legs would be healed, tumours would fall off, and so on. They all had one thing besides sickness in common: they had FAITH. They really believed in Jesus' power to save, heal and deliver.

And so Matthew reports that they were healed. The word in the original Greek is actually a lot more exciting. Instead of the usual Greek verb for heal, *sozo*, Matthew uses a much rarer word, *diasozo*. This is a combination of *sozo*, to heal, and *dia*, meaning thoroughly or completely. *Diasozo* means to cure completely, to restore perfectly, to heal totally. What Matthew is talking about here is total cures. In Gennesaret, the crowds reached out to Jesus and just one touch changed everything – totally, perfectly, completely.

Don't you just long for a *diasozo* move of God like that today? For that to happen, we will need to be desperate enough to grab hold of the King as he passes by. In short, we will need to have faith in God. We will need to have fighting faith.

Time to Reach Out to Jesus

In 2005 I was preaching on the subject of this book: 'One touch from the King changes everything.' As we started to sing a song of worship, a lady on the front row was reflecting on this idea of the King's transforming touch. She had a serious disability caused by a horrific car accident twenty years earlier. As a result of her injuries she had not been able to lift her left hand above the level of her shoulder for two decades. Her left arm was locked in position, as if it was in a sling.

Remembering the story of the woman reaching out to touch Jesus' garment, she decided that she was going to reach out to God. Desperate for her healing, she started to sing praises to the Lord and stretch out her disabled arm to heaven. Suddenly she found she was able to do what she'd been unable to do since her accident. She raised her left hand so that her arm was completely outstretched above her head. For the first time in two decades she was able to raise both arms in adoration. As she did so, her husband standing next to her saw what was happening and fell to his seat, weeping.

No one had asked her to come to the front to receive. No one was praying for her at the time with the laying-on of hands. She simply reached out to touch the King. Two days later she shared her testimony with the whole church. The church family – who knew the lady well – broke into applause and shared in her joy.

I love the way Bishop Joseph Garlington puts it in his amazing song, 'Just one touch':

This is your moment; don't wait
This is your hour; press in
Only reach out; it's time to receive
Look to me now and only believe.

I believe God is calling those in need to stretch out their hand to touch the King and to do so with fighting faith. I also believe that God is calling those who pray for the sick to do so with the same kind of fighting faith. In Mark chapter 3, Jesus heals a man with a withered arm. Mark reports in verse 5 (NLT): 'He said to the man, "Reach out your hand." The man reached out his hand, and it became normal again!' The man had to play his part by stretching out his arm in faith and obedience. Jesus then played his part by healing the man miraculously. Healing miracles are God's work, to be sure. But we have a part to play in the process. We are to exhibit fighting faith unless and until we are told otherwise by the Lord.

Dare to reach out your hand
into the darkness, to pull
another hand into the light.

Norman B. Rice

Chapter 4

The King of Hearts

His name is Francesco. He comes from a very rich family and everyone loves him; he is handsome, wealthy and charming. He is often found in a crowd of young people addicted to pleasure and parties. He has just been to war as a soldier and been captured – but as a man of great means he has been able to secure his release after a year.

One day, now aged 25, he is riding a horse down a country road. Francesco sees a man ahead of him. He hears the sound of a bell being rung and the words 'Unclean, unclean.' To his horror, Francesco realises that it is a leper. He is dressed in a filthy garment pieced together from bits of sacking. The bell he has rung is hanging by a cord from his neck. His body is emaciated and half his face has been eaten away.

Francesco is appalled. Since he was a young boy he has been terrified of lepers – appalled by their appearance and disgusted by the smell of their rotting flesh. Francesco could ride on. There is no one else around. The two are alone in the stillness of the countryside, on a deserted road surrounded by olive trees. As he prepares to lift the reins of his horse, he sees the very ornate gloves he is wearing. Suddenly he is overwhelmed by the contrast between him and the leper.

Francesco's heart begins to change. For months he has been stirred by a sense that there has to be more than the life he is pursuing. This deep sentiment grips him again. As Francesco looks once more upon him, the leper reaches out his arm. His hand is just a stump. He is begging for money so that he can eat.

Something happens in Francesco's soul as the gesture is made. He dismounts and walks towards the man, opening his purse as he goes. He takes out a silver coin and puts it in the remains of the man's hand. He battles with his nausea at the stench. But then he tenderly takes hold of the man's hand and kisses it. The two men reach towards each other and embrace. In a decisive moment of revelation, Francesco realises that this man is a person made in the image of God – and that God embraces all people.

He remounts his horse and begins to ride off. He feels as if he is somehow transformed. He turns to give the leper a wave, but as he turns he cannot see the man anywhere. He has disappeared.

That is the turning point. From then on Francesco gives his life to serving the poor. Today he is known as St Francis. His transformation was a long process, but that moment when he touched a leper changed everything. On his deathbed many years later St Francis recalled the encounter as the crowning moment of his conversion: 'What seemed bitter to me was changed into sweetness of soul and body.' Mother Teresa once said, 'That was the beginning of St Francis. That act of surrender *made* St Francis . . . After that he was ready to give anything!'

Touching the Untouchables

It is hard not to be moved and challenged by stories like this. When people like Francesco learn to touch the untouchables out of the love of God, it sends a compelling signal. It demonstrates that same kindness revealed in God himself, who stepped down from the majesty of heaven, took on human flesh and washed our dirty feet. Every time a person of position humbles themselves for the sake of the vulnerable, something of God's journey from heaven to earth is enacted once again in the midst of us. It never ceases to engage our imaginations.

One of the most enduring photographs of the 1990s showed Princess Diana in a hospital, holding the hand of a patient dying of HIV/AIDS. Diana was known for her compassion and was nicknamed 'the Queen of Hearts'. Her attitude towards HIV/AIDS sufferers was summed up in her remark, 'HIV does not make people dangerous to know, so you can shake their hands and give them a hug. Heaven knows, they need it.' When Diana held the hand of that HIV/AIDS patient, the photograph and the TV pictures went all around the world. Andrew Parkis, chief executive of the Princess of Wales Memorial Fund, said the image 'shattered the stigma, prejudice and fear that surrounded HIV/AIDS in the early days'. It was truly a defining moment in the 1990s.

It is well known that Princess Diana's inspiration was Mother Teresa. Mother Teresa was known throughout the world as an Angel of Mercy. She was famous particularly for her love of the 'untouchables' in India. She once said these challenging words: 'Let us touch the dying, the poor, the lonely and the unwanted according to the graces we have received and let us not be ashamed or slow to do the humble work.'

Mother Teresa in turn caught her vision from Jesus, the most compassionate person in history. She once said of Jesus:

He is the Life that I want to live,
He is the Light that I want to radiate.
He is the Way to the Father.
He is the Love with which I want to love.
He is the Joy that I want to share.
He is the Peace that I want to sow.
Jesus is Everything to me.
Without Him, I can do nothing.

It was the inspiring example of the love of Jesus that led Mother Teresa to set up one of the first ever homes for AIDS sufferers. By the end of her life her sisters had established 450 centres for the world's most poor, sick and unwanted people.

Jesus and the Leper

Diana may have been the Queen of Hearts but Jesus of Nazareth was the King of Hearts. More than anyone else,

Jesus believed in touching the untouchables with his Father's love. He touched people who were regarded as impure in his own religion. He touched the dead, the unclean, the leprous, the demonised, and so on. As Bono of U2 once said:

> If Jesus were on earth . . . he'd be with people suffering from AIDS. These are the new lepers. If you want to find out where Jesus would be hanging out, it'll always be with the lepers.

At the end of the first chapter of Mark's Gospel we find Jesus performing one of his first healing miracles – the cleansing of a leper. We read in verses 40–45:

> Now a leper came to Him, imploring Him, kneeling down to Him and saying to Him, 'If You are willing, You can make me clean.' Then Jesus, moved with compassion, stretched out His hand and touched him, and said to him, 'I am willing; be cleansed.' As soon as He had spoken, immediately the leprosy left him, and he was cleansed. And He strictly warned him and sent him away at once, and said to him, 'See that you say nothing to anyone; but go your way, show yourself to the priest, and offer for your cleansing those things which Moses commanded, as a testimony to them.' However, he went out and began to proclaim it freely, and to spread the matter, so that Jesus could no longer openly enter the city, but was outside in deserted places; and they came to Him from every direction.

This is a truly remarkable moment in the unfolding drama of Jesus' ministry. Right at the start of his work, Jesus touches a leper and commands his healing. This would have shocked the eyewitnesses who saw this incident. It would have shocked the first readers of Mark's Gospel. It is an act even more striking than Princess Diana holding the hand of an HIV/AIDS sufferer.

Of all the diseases that Jesus confronted, leprosy was the most feared in his day. Leprosy was – and is – an infectious condition caused by a bacterium known as *mycobacterium leprae*. This bacterium results in disfiguration of the body or the skin. The parts of a person's body affected by the bacterium become distorted, twisted and useless. In Jesus' time this resulted in a long and lonely death that often would take years.

In the first century there was no known medical treatment for leprosy. The fact that it was contagious meant that lepers had to live apart from everyone else. As soon as someone was diagnosed as a leper their clothes were burned and their house destroyed. They were excluded from the Temple and from normal society. They had to live outside city walls and away from their families. They had to wear torn clothes so that their illness was clearly visible. When anyone came near, lepers were to shout 'Unclean, unclean' to warn them. By the time of Jesus, the Jews had added further quarantine procedures. A healthy person had to stand an agreed distance away from a leper, depending on the direction of the wind.

No disease caused as much traumatic segregation as leprosy. The usual reaction to seeing a leper was either to throw stones at them or to run as fast as possible in the opposite direction. Lepers lived in isolation. Food was often hard to come by. The only comfort for a leper was the company of other lepers. A leper certainly wouldn't normally dream of approaching a priest or a Rabbi in the way the man does in this story in Mark chapter 1.

The purity code of the Temple emphasised exclusion. These purity laws established a fixed boundary around people and places. The clear message was, 'If you're unclean, you can't come in.' The lepers were the most unclean of all. The leper was the most stigmatised of all people. He or she stood at the opposite end of the spectrum from the priests who served in the sacred courts of the Temple in Jerusalem.

Jesus ministered in this world of exclusion zones. But he adopted a different stance. He did not separate himself from lepers. In fact, he reached out his hand and blessed them. Jesus touched the untouchables. While the priests in the Temple regarded lepers as social outcasts, Jesus regarded them as human beings made in the image of God. While the religious leaders looked on them with condemnation, Jesus looked on them with compassion.

What Jesus did was to remove the walls of exclusion and look with kindness on those who were ostracised. He ministered as a prophet on the periphery. He was truly the Messiah of the margins and the marginalised. By his very example he sent the clearest signal that the Kingdom of God is an open set – a place of mercy and welcome for those whom society treats as outcasts. While many of his contemporaries advocated exclusion, Jesus advocated embrace.

The healing miracles of Jesus – especially those involving lepers – reveal a Messiah who demonstrates a very robust and costly kind of love. The love that Jesus showed was not some brief Hollywood encounter, nor was it a smouldering magazine pose. The love that Jesus demonstrated was the look of kindness and the squeeze of a hand . . . the gesture that said, 'You're accepted, you're included, you're not forgotten; the Father loves you.'

One Touch from the King

When Jesus met the leper walking towards him, the most significant thing he did was touch him. Normally, such touch was forbidden. If you touched a leper even accidentally you had to go through a rigorous process of separation and washing. But Jesus reached out to the leper who knelt in front of him. Most probably Jesus touched the man's head or shoulder. Wherever the leper was touched, the likelihood is that this was the first contact he had felt since contracting the disease. The touch alone signalled mercy, kindness and inclusion. But it also signalled healing, freedom and wholeness. As Jesus touched him and spoke words of life over him, the leper was immediately healed. Truly, one touch changed everything.

It is interesting at this point to compare a story from the Old Testament – the story of the healing of Naaman in 2 Kings, chapter 5. Naaman was a Syrian general who had caused Israel a lot of suffering. He had somehow caught leprosy and was subsequently told of a prophet in Israel called Elisha who had a gift of healing. This information came to him via a young Israelite girl whom he had captured and given as a slave to his wife. Hearing this, Naaman goes to Israel to visit the prophet. When he arrives, Elisha doesn't come out to meet Naaman in person but sends a messenger instructing the general to wash seven times in the River Jordan. The general is upset about this for two reasons. First he thinks that the Jordan is a much dirtier river than the ones he would have chosen in Syria. Secondly, he thinks Elisha should have come in person and prayed for him with elaborate hand gestures. This is what the storyteller says in 2 Kings 5:11 (NLT):

> Naaman became angry and stalked away. 'I thought he would surely come out to meet me!' he said. 'I expected him to wave his hand over the leprosy and call on the name of the LORD his God and heal me!'

Naaman subsequently relents and washes in the Jordan, whereupon he is instantly healed. As a result, Naaman acknowledges that Israel's God is the one true God.

What's so interesting here is the difference between Elisha's way of operating and that revealed by Jesus. Elisha doesn't go in person to meet the leper. He sends a messenger instead. Furthermore, Elisha doesn't reach out his hand to the leper. He sends a message to the general to wash seven times in the Jordan. How different from Jesus. Jesus meets the leper himself and he reaches out to touch him. Unlike Elisha, Jesus risks physical contact with the leper. Moved by a divine and profound compassion, Jesus reached out to the man.

And this touch was more than an act of kindness. It was the instrument of divine healing. As Jesus laid his hand upon the leper and spoke a word of command, God's miracle-working power came to the leper, bringing about instant transformation. And note what happens as soon as the leper is healed: Jesus gives him two instructions. The first is to tell no one. The reason for this is fairly obvious: the healing of a leper would have been unheard of in Israel at that time. News of such a miracle would have caused Jesus untold trouble in terms of public acclaim. The second is to go and show himself to the priest in the Temple and to submit to the regulations prescribed for this eventuality. This is an elaborate procedure that had to be undertaken before a person could be readmitted into the community.

It is not hard to imagine the scene when the leper arrives at the Temple. He goes into the outer courts and presents his case to the priest on duty. You can imagine the commotion. People at the time of Jesus regarded the miraculous healing of leprosy as impossible. No one in Israel had seen a leper healed since the time of Elisha, a thousand years before. The priests that day must have had great trouble just finding the scroll on which the 'Leper Cleansing Rituals' were written! When they did, it must have been covered in dust from centuries of disuse. Truly a miracle had occurred that was beyond their experience or their expectation.

Mercy and Miracles

The clear lesson from all of this is that one touch changes everything. But it's important to note what kind of touch. The touch ministered by Jesus is a touch of love as well as power. It is a touch involving mercy as well as miracles. We are going to need both today as we minister to the leprosies of our age.

First of all, we are going to need mercy. The more I look at the King's touch in the ministry of Jesus, the more I am struck by the kindness of that touch. So often the Gospel writers talk about how Jesus was moved by compassion. In the original language the word refers to a visceral feeling of empathy resulting in practical acts of love. Jesus was deeply moved by the plight of the sick and those in need. He was particularly affected by the terrible circumstances of the lepers.

If we want to tackle the leprosies of our age we are going to have to recapture this Messianic virtue of mercy. Mother Teresa's legacy is one of mercy. That is why her co-workers are called 'Sisters of Mercy'. Mercy is the number one characteristic of Mother Teresa's life. As she once said, 'I see God in every human being. When I wash the leper's wounds

I feel I am nursing the Lord himself. Is it not a beautiful experience?' On another occasion she said this:

> Be kind and merciful. Let no one ever come to you without coming away better and happier. Be the living expression of God's kindness: kindness in your face, kindness in your eyes, kindness in your smile, kindness in your warm greeting. In the slums we are the light of God's kindness to the poor. To children, to the poor, to all who suffer and are lonely, give always a happy smile – Give them not only your care, but also your heart.

I believe more and more that compassion, kindness and mercy are essential if we want to minister the King's touch today.

Earlier in this book I mentioned the ministry of Dr David Carr at Solihull Renewal Centre. Having met David, I visited his church for one of their Tuesday evening healing meetings. About a thousand people turned up from all over the country, many in great need. What struck me so powerfully – as David prayed for all of them at the front – was his extraordinary compassion. He not only touched the sick, he embraced them. He held them in his arms and wept over them as he prayed for them. Never have I seen such mercy and kindness in the healing ministry. No wonder this church has become the place of great miracles.

And it is miracles that we need too. It is not enough simply to minister the mercy of God. There must be signs and wonders too. Jesus showed great kindness to the sick, yes. But he also did something about their condition! He healed them. Jesus ministered in both the power and the love of God. He performed miracles in the lives of those who received his mercy.

So it is important to stress signs, wonders and miracles as well as compassion, mercy and kindness. It is not enough to show mercy to those suffering from the leprosies of our age. We must also believe that God can do miracles too. If nothing is impossible for the Lord, then even HIV/AIDS can be healed.

A friend of mine called Marc Dupont recently encouraged me by telling me of an incident when God used him in the healing of a man with HIV/AIDS. This is what he wrote:

> I prayed for a man who was definitely healed of advanced HIV/ AIDS. He lived in Orebro, Sweden. He had been a backslidden Christian who had contracted AIDS from a needle. After getting very sick he recommitted his life to the Lord, as did his girlfriend. I went with a friend to his flat to pray for him. The man was so sick he could not leave his flat. He had been told that he had a month to live. As we prayed for him we felt the presence of the Lord very powerfully, although he did not feel anything at the time. I was later informed that from that time on he completely recovered.

This is not the only time Marc has seen the miraculous healing of people with HIV/AIDS. In the last few months he has been witnessing an increase in such miracles. Here is another example:

> A month ago I ministered at Metro Church South in Cleveland, Ohio. It had been announced the week before that I would pray for people with cancer and serious diseases. A man named Chris came from another church for the meetings. I did not know he had been HIV positive for several years. As I prayed for him I was led by the Lord to pray for cleansing of his blood. Later that week the man asked his doctor to prescribe fresh blood tests. However, he was in for a surprise. Chris's doctor does not know what has happened to the disease!

Testimonies like these are an important reminder to us that we need to use the gift of miracles, not just the gift of mercy. Both of these grace gifts are mentioned by the Apostle Paul. Mercy is mentioned in the list of the gifts in Romans 12. The gift of miracles is referred to in 1 Corinthians 12. Mercy is vital. But so is the gift of miracles. Indeed, we should remember Jesus' mandate to his followers in Matthew 10:7–8 (NLT):

Go and announce to them that the Kingdom of Heaven is near. Heal the sick, raise the dead, cure those with leprosy, and cast out demons. Give as freely as you have received!

Jesus evidently believed that his disciples had the authority and power to heal lepers. He expected them to minister in miracles as well as in mercy. We who are called to pray 'Your Kingdom come' must usher in God's rule not just through acts of kindness but also through acts of life-changing power. We are not – in the final analysis – social workers, even if we have a responsibility for social transformation. We are ministers of the Good News of Jesus, which means communicating the message of his love in both acts of mercy and miraculous works.

Out of Africa

The church's role in Uganda offers a great example to us of this combination of mercy and miracles. Since the 1970s, when Idi Amin tried to convert the nation to Islam, Uganda has been turning to Christianity. The growth of the church has been phenomenal, not least through its preaching of the Gospel using acts of service and prayer for miracles. It is estimated today that one-fifth of Uganda's 26 million inhabitants are followers of Jesus. Church buildings accommodating congregations of ten thousand are common.

A key moment in the transformation of this nation came in 1991 when Balaki Kirya (the Minister of State Security) called area pastors and told them that the government was now handing over the HIV/AIDS crisis to the church. At that time it was anticipated that, if the trends continued, just under one-third of the population would be dead by the year 2000 and a similar number infected with HIV. The church instantly mobilised and began a campaign of information (disseminated through local churches) and serving the vulnerable. The church also began communicating a message of abstinence. Today, as a result, HIV/AIDS prevalence among adults is roughly 5%, not the anticipated 30+%. Thanks to this extraordinary army of Christian volunteers, Uganda has halted a runaway killer.

Uganda's success in this area is unrivalled. But it has come not just through the showing of mercy – involving medical care – but also through the power of miracles. In Uganda people have frequently been healed of HIV/AIDS when they have been prayed for in Jesus' name. In fact, the Christian message is often referred to as 'the miracle Gospel' in Uganda.

To quote one example, Fally Kuteesa (a leader at Christian Life Church in Kampala) was healed of HIV/AIDS. She believed that God was going to heal her miraculously. One day she had a vision and saw her name with these words next to it: 'negative, negative, negative'. The next day she went for her twentieth set of tests and was declared 'negative'. She was healed! Over one hundred people were reported healed in the evangelistic rallies led by Deo Balabyekubo between 1990 and 1995. He led three sets of forty-day fasts, praying for God to deal supernaturally with the HIV/AIDS pandemic. After Deo's death in 1995, Bishop Grivas Musisi took over the ministry. In the very next rally more than three hundred people were healed of HIV/AIDS and their cures verified by doctors!

So miracles are needed as well as mercy. Of course, not everyone prayed for is healed. Bishop Musisi himself has said, 'We realised that God heals, but also that he may choose not to heal.' Nevertheless, the Gospel preached in Uganda has been a Gospel of miracles as well as mercy. This message, communicated by a growing church that the dictator Idi Amin tried so hard to destroy, is a big part of the secret to the unparalleled success that Uganda has had in fighting HIV/AIDS.

The Leprosy of Our Age

Why have a chapter on HIV/AIDS in a book about the miraculous touch of God? There are a number of big reasons for this. The first is simply that we can't afford to ignore the issue. It is now certain that HIV/AIDS represents perhaps the greatest challenge to the world today. In 2006 the lead singer of the band U2 addressed the National Prayer Breakfast in Washington DC. This was attended by some of the most powerful men and women in the world, including the US President. Bono used this opportunity to give a rousing and heartfelt call to act on behalf of Africa, and in particular in the fight against the raging fire of HIV/AIDS. He described HIV/AIDS as the leprosy of our age. He ended his remarkable speech by uttering these haunting words:

> I truly believe that when the history books are written, our age will be remembered for three things: the war on terror, the digital revolution, and what we did – or did not do – to put the fire out in Africa. History, like God, is watching what we do.

Bono's words are not just rhetoric. They are reality. Consider the following statistics reported by Tearfund:

- Five people die of AIDS every minute, more than seven thousand people every day; one in five of these deaths is a child under 15
- Every day another 14,000 people are infected with HIV; one in seven of these is a child under 15
- 600,000 children are newly infected every year, mostly via their parents
- The number of children orphaned as a result of HIV and AIDS is nearly 15 million; by 2010 this number will exceed 25 million
- 80% of the children orphaned by AIDS live in sub-Saharan Africa
- 39 million people in the world are living with HIV; 2.3 million of these are children
- In 25 years AIDS has killed more than 20 million people worldwide

AIDS is on course to become the most catastrophic pandemic in human history. It is a global disaster. No one can afford to ignore the facts any more.

HIV/AIDS is a fact of twenty-first-century life that cannot be avoided. It is significant that Rick Warren (author of the hugely successful book *The Purpose Driven Life* and leader of one of the largest churches in the USA) has made the fight against AIDS his premier message in recent days. At a conference in Toronto in 2006, Rick and Kay Warren said this:

> The solution to eliminating the threat of HIV/AIDS is not education, it is transformation. That involves saving sex for marriage, training men to respect women, offering treatment through churches and encouraging individuals to pledge themselves to one partner. I believe that faith, ethics and morals play an important role in the fight against HIV/AIDS. I am not a scientist, a medical professional or activist. I am a pastor, whose motives are different. I love people, and I have a Saviour named Jesus who said, 'Love your neighbour as yourself.'

The second reason for having a chapter on HIV/AIDS is that many believe that it is in this area that Jesus would be ministering much of his time were he physically present in the world today. Dr Jo Lusi says this:

> If we ask, 'What would Jesus do and where would he go in the 21st century?' he would be doing home-care visits in the slums to people dying of AIDS, and he would be showing people how a godly way of life protects life.

The good news is that the churches in Africa are now on the front line of people tackling the HIV/AIDS crisis. Largely unseen and unrecognised, millions of Christian volunteers are operating under the radar of their government's attention, bringing God's love to sufferers in a practical and powerful way. This army of volunteers is working very long hours, showing God's kindness to orphans and his care for the sick. With precious little support from political sources, these community volunteers are dispelling the prejudice around HIV and AIDS, teaching a message of sexual abstinence and fidelity, supporting and praying for the sick and fighting trends such as parent-to-child transmission of HIV. The church is hearing the call to be where Jesus would be if he were physically present in the world.

Showing Kindness to Others

There is a third reason for including a chapter on HIV/AIDS . . . and here we need to go to one of the most challenging passages in the Bible.

In Isaiah chapter 58 God chastises his people for fasting in an insincere way. They have been acting piously in appearance, but in reality their hearts are far from right with God. In particular, they have been speaking negatively against one another and they have been neglecting to help the victims of economic and social injustice. In the face of this hypocrisy God speaks bluntly through his prophet in verse 4 (NLT):

> What good is fasting when you keep on fighting and quarrelling?
> This kind of fasting will never get you anywhere with me.

In addition, the prophet utters this warning in verses 6–7:

> No, the kind of fasting I want calls you to free those who are wrongly imprisoned and to stop oppressing those who work for you. Treat them fairly and give them what they earn. I want you to share your food with the hungry and to welcome poor wanderers into your homes. Give clothes to those who need them, and do not hide from relatives who need your help.

What's going on here? In a nutshell, the people of God have forgotten the virtue of kindness. They have stopped being kind to one another within the community. And they have stopped being kind to the poor as well. In the face of such unkindness, God encourages his people to engage in two new types of fasting: a fast from negativity and a fast from oppression. He promises the following rewards in verses 8–9:

> If you do these things, your salvation will come like the dawn. Yes, your healing will come quickly. Your godliness will lead

you forward, and the glory of the LORD will protect you from behind. Then when you call, the LORD will answer. 'Yes, I am here,' he will quickly reply.

I am convinced that God wants his people to become more kind, merciful and compassionate – to each other and to the vulnerable, the poor, the sick. If we want to minister the touch of the King, then we will need to discover God's heart of compassion. We will need to exercise the gift of mercy. We will need to be kind. As Leo Buscaglia says, 'Too often we underestimate the power of a touch, a smile, a kind word, a listening ear, an honest compliment, or the smallest act of caring, all of which have the potential to turn a life around.'

Truly, one kind touch can change everything.

> Have a heart that never
> hardens, and a temper that
> never tires, and a touch that
> never hurts.
>
> Charles Dickens

Chapter 5

God's Touch Through You

No Christian should underestimate the power of just one touch. When God puts his big hand on our little hands, all things are possible.

Consider the origin of the work of the Holy Spirit in the twentieth century. The last hundred years have seen the most dramatic movements of God's Holy Spirit since the first century.

The first of these came in the first decade of the twentieth century. At a small, run-down mission building in Los Angeles something history-making occurred. God poured out his Spirit on a group of spiritually hungry people. Many thousands were saved, healed and set free in the subsequent years. Dramatic miracles occurred. People were sent all over the world as missionaries as the Azusa Street mission became the birthplace of the Pentecostal movement. Today, there are some 63 million people who call themselves Pentecostal in various denominations around the world, and that number is growing every year.

The second wave hit the historic denominations in the 1960s, particularly the Anglican and Roman Catholic Churches. While this wave also launched some 'house' churches too, it was in the mainline churches that this work of the Spirit was most dramatically felt. All over the world the historic churches began to experience the work of the Spirit. The gifts of the Spirit – including tongues, healing and prophecy – were exercised in these churches as they had been in the Pentecostal ones. Today, the Charismatics number around

175 million, and that number too is growing. As in the case of the first wave, much of this growth is evangelistic.

In the 1970s a third wave broke. This has created a vast number who are neither Pentecostals nor renewed members of the historic churches. These 'neo-Charismatics' belong to independent churches. They too have a marked emphasis on God's empowering presence. They too expect and witness miracles. The neo-Charismatics number about 295 million and are growing.

David Barrett estimates that around 795 million Christians have been birthed out of the outpouring of the Holy Spirit at Azusa Street in 1906. All three waves continue to create massive expansion. Some 25,000 new believers are added every day, 9 million every year – one-third being brand new converts. In addition, every continent has been touched by these three moves. All three waves have fuelled a passion for mission and created many mission agencies. This has not been without cost; Christians affected by these three waves are among the most persecuted in the world. Nevertheless, the impact of the twentieth-century moves of God has been so great that Pentecostal Christianity is now considered the fourth stream of Christianity – alongside the Protestant, the Roman Catholic and the Orthodox streams.

So the effect of what happened at Azusa Street in 1906 should not be underestimated. It is massive.

And it's precisely at this point that we see once again the dynamic potential of just one touch.

In tracing the origins of these three waves Vinson Synon goes back before 1906, to 1 January 1901. On that day a young woman called Agnes Ozman was filled with the Holy Spirit and began speaking in tongues. This occurred when Charles Parham – Ozman's teacher at Topeka Bible School in Kansas – laid hands on her. This is how Parham records the moment:

> I laid my hands upon her and prayed. I had scarcely completed three dozen sentences when a glory fell upon her, a halo seemed to surround her head and face, and she began speaking the Chinese language and was unable to speak English for three days.

Synon describes Ozman as the first Pentecostal of the twentieth century and traces the 1906 outpouring to this moment. It was significantly described as 'the touch felt around the world'. What God did through the hands of Charles Parham on New Year's Day at the start of the twentieth century was ultimately global in its impact. It is an abiding example of how one touch of the King can change everything. It is also a graphic example of how God does amazing things *through human hands*. As theologian Frederick Buechner eloquently puts it:

> The life I touch for good or ill will touch another life, and that in turn another, until who knows where the trembling stops or in what far place my touch will be felt.

In this final chapter we look at how God works through our hands to minister a touch that can change everything.

An Apostolic Prayer

When God poured out his Spirit on Azusa Street, this work was quickly described with the adjective 'Pentecostal', harking back to the Day of Pentecost 1,900 years before.

On the Day of Pentecost (described in Acts chapter 2), God poured out his Holy Spirit upon the first Christians and they were filled with mighty power. Peter preached a message to the Jewish pilgrims assembled in Jerusalem for the Feast of Pentecost and three thousand people became Christians at the end of that, his first, sermon. These new converts were baptised and the church subsequently formed (Acts 2:42–47).

In Acts chapter 3 Peter and John are seen going to the Temple at the set hour of prayer at 3pm. They are confronted by a man who has been lame for over forty years. He cries out to them for money. Peter doesn't have any money but he speaks a word of command and then reaches out to the man to help him up. This is how Luke records the moment in Acts 3:7–8 (NLT):

Then Peter took the lame man by the right hand and helped him up. And as he did, the man's feet and anklebones were healed and strengthened. He jumped up, stood on his feet, and began to walk! Then, walking, leaping, and praising God, he went into the Temple with them.

This great miracle results in both celebration and controversy. The man celebrates his new mobility but the religious rulers in Jerusalem become mad at what Peter and John have done. In Acts chapter 4 we read that they arrest the two apostles and have them thrown in jail overnight. The next day they hold a hearing and ask them by whose authority they have healed the man. This leads to a very bold declaration about the name of Jesus. The religious leaders tell the apostles that they are not to speak of Jesus' name any longer, but Peter and John refuse to comply. Not knowing how to punish them, the leaders are forced to set the apostles free.

As soon as they rejoin the rest of the church all the believers break into prayer. They worship God for his sovereign power and authority, especially over those earthly rulers who think they are the ones in control. Then they conclude their prayer with this request in Acts 4:29–30:

> Now, Lord, look on their threats, and grant to Your servants that with all boldness they may speak Your word, by stretching out Your hand to heal, and that signs and wonders may be done through the name of Your holy Servant Jesus.

These early Christians ask God to stretch out his hand to heal and to perform signs, wonders and miracles. This is a simple but heartfelt prayer. But when was it answered? When did God stretch out his hand and perform miracles? The answer is found in the next chapter, Acts 5. In verse 12 Luke reports:

> And through the hands of the apostles many signs and wonders were done among the people.

Here is the answer to the apostolic prayer of Acts 4. The big hand of God worked through the little hands of his people. God stretches out his hand when we stretch out ours!

The Big Hand of God

The phrase 'the hand of the Lord' is frequently found in the Bible. It always refers to the mighty power of God. So we read in Ezekiel 1:3 (NLT):

> The LORD gave a message to me, Ezekiel son of Buzi, a priest, there beside the River Kebar in the land of the Babylonians, and I felt the hand of the LORD take hold of me.

Sometimes the expression refers to God's work of creation. Isaiah 64:8 (NLT) says:

> And yet, LORD, you are our Father. We are the clay, and you are the potter. We are all formed by your hand.

Sometimes the expression refers to the work of God in judgement. Isaiah 9:17 (NIV) says:

> Yet for all this, his anger is not turned away, his hand is still upraised.

At other times the expression refers to God's mercy and forgiveness. So Psalm 37:23–24 (NLT) says:

> The steps of the godly are directed by the LORD.
> He delights in every detail of their lives.
> Though they stumble, they will not fall,
> for the LORD holds them by the hand.

When the apostles lead the early church in prayer in Acts chapter 4 they ask God to stretch out his hand to heal the sick. In this instance the hand of the Lord refers to the miracle-working power of God – specifically to God's ability to perform signs and wonders.

Throughout this book I have been emphasising time and again that one touch from the King changes everything.

I believe that God stretches out his hand today. He does this independently of us. And he does this through us. On occasions, God acts independently of human agency. He stretches out his hand and heals the sick without anyone else's help. I have given examples of that in this book. On other occasions (and this is the rule rather than the exception), God uses our hands when he stretches out his hand. In other words, when he wants to do a miracle in the life of a sick person, most frequently he will do that as we stretch out our hands and pray for them.

These are days in which we are being called to pray the apostolic prayer of Acts 4 – to pray for a revelation of the hand of the Lord. The hand of the Lord is going to be revealed more and more, especially as we stretch out our hands and pray for the sick. Putting it simply, it's going to be like a clock when the big hand and the little hand come together in perfect alignment.

The touch of the King occurs most often when God's hand and ours line up, in God's perfect timing, to bring about a touch that changes everything. This is what happened in the Book of Acts. The church prayed for God's hand to be outstretched in Acts 4. Then the apostles stretched out their hands in Acts 5. All this reminds us of the great value that Jesus places upon us as his human agents. As Teresa of Avila once said:

> Christ has no body now on earth but yours, no hands but yours, no feet but yours; yours are the eyes through which Christ's compassion looks out onto the world, yours are the feet with which he is to go about doing good and yours are the hands with which he is to bless now.

Restoring Apostolic Christianity

I have a conviction on my heart: these are days in which the Holy Spirit is raising up a truly apostolic church. What do I mean by an 'apostolic church'? The root from which we get the word 'apostle' is a Greek word meaning 'send'.

An apostle is literally someone sent out, in particular as the pioneer of a new Gospel ministry in places untouched by the Gospel. Apostolic Christianity is accordingly pioneering Christianity. It is the faith that sees no limits, no boundaries, and works for increase in terms of the Kingdom of God. Apostolic Christianity is the kind of Christianity we see in the New Testament. It is a radical, adventurous Christianity that seeks to work outwards from vibrant Kingdom centres into the earth – locally, regionally, nationally and globally. Apostolic Christianity is a Christianity of expansion.

Perhaps the best New Testament model for this kind of apostolic church is the church of Antioch established at the end of Acts chapter 11. In the first part of Acts the church is too focused on Jerusalem and on a 'Jews-only' congregation. Jesus had told the apostles that they were to be his witnesses beyond Jerusalem, in Judea, Samaria, and to the ends of the earth (Acts 1:8). The Jerusalem church had not obeyed that call and so God allowed persecution to come. In Acts 8:1 this persecution causes the church to scatter from its gathered centre in Jerusalem and to disperse into its worldwide mission field. It is as a result of this scattering process that the church in Antioch is born. As Luke records in Acts 11:19–21 (NIV):

> Now those who had been scattered by the persecution in connection with Stephen travelled as far as Phoenicia, Cyprus and Antioch, telling the message only to Jews. Some of them, however, men from Cyprus and Cyrene, went to Antioch and began to speak to Greeks also, telling them the good news about the Lord Jesus. The Lord's hand was with them, and a great number of people believed and turned to the Lord.

Notice here how the persecution is said to cause a scattering of God's people. This is not a negative but a positive thing! God had wanted his church to be both gathered and dispersed – to be gathered in Jerusalem and at the same time dispersed without limits or boundaries. Even after this persecution has hit the church, it's interesting to see how some of the early Christians still don't get it. If you look carefully at the words above you'll see that some of the Jewish Christians who had been scattered were still only sharing the Gospel with the Jews. Others were more radical. They went to the city of Antioch in Syria and started witnessing to non-Jews. And it says that as they engaged in this cross-cultural mission, 'the hand of the Lord was with them'. The power of God was upon those who engaged in a truly apostolic expression of Christianity. Those who were prepared to be sent beyond the existing boundaries knew God's favour. Consequently they witnessed many miracles – miracles of conversion, healing, deliverance and the like.

The truth is that God loves this apostolic, pioneering spirit in his people. He loves that entrepreneurial Kingdom mentality that seeks to go beyond the territorial limits so often set up by religious people. In many places God is stirring up an apostolic zeal in churches, causing them to break out of their restriction zones and to take the Good News of Jesus – with mercy and miracles – to places and people that have not heard this life-changing message. As that happens, 'the hand of the Lord' is revealed. It is revealed in many ways, but one of the most significant ways is that healing touch of the King that changes everything.

Handshakes and Napkins

One of the hallmarks of a genuinely apostolic expression of Christianity is the way in which the big hand of God works through the small hands of God's people. As with the church in Antioch, such Christians know the hand of the Lord is with them. They don't just see healings. They see extraordinary signs, wonders and miracles.

The church in Antioch is therefore a great model for us. From Acts 11 onwards, this church becomes the missionary headquarters for the earliest church. From this centre the Gospel goes out to the world. This occurs particularly through the Apostle Paul, who is sent out from Antioch on three missionary journeys. On one of these he visits the city of Ephesus (in modern Turkey). Here Luke records that there were extraordinary miracles as the apostle preached in that city. In Acts 19:11–12 he says:

> Now God worked unusual miracles by the hands of Paul, so that even handkerchiefs or aprons were brought from his body to the sick, and the diseases left them and the evil spirits went out of them.

Notice the phrase 'unusual miracles'. That is in itself unusual. The first time I saw that, I asked myself, 'How can there be such a thing as an "unusual" miracle?' Miracles are by definition unusual. They are exceptional circumstances in which God intervenes supernaturally in our world, causing awe and wonder in the lives of those who witness them. In this light the idea of 'unusual miracles' seems like saying the same thing twice.

I have since realised that this is a little pedantic! Luke clearly saw miracles in the life of the Apostle Paul, and he saw them often. There were some fairly typical ways in which these happened. What Luke saw in Ephesus was miracles performed in unconventional ways. This was not the more usual approach of Paul laying hands on the sick and issuing a word of command to the sickness. This was a case of Paul blessing handkerchiefs and aprons and these being taken to the sick and used as vehicles of extraordinary power. Now that was an unusual method!

It could well be that we are living in days when we are going to see not just miracles but 'unusual miracles'. That thought has occurred to me particularly as a result of the testimony I shared in the introduction to this book. When it came to Hank's healing and salvation, two things played a significant part: a handshake at the end of a church service and a prophecy written on a napkin. As a result of these two things, Hank's world was turned upside down. Speaking for myself, that was not something 'usual'!

As we transition into a more apostolic kind of Christianity – focused on the lost – I believe we need to gear ourselves up for 'unusual miracles'. We are going to see the hand of the Lord, as the Christians did in Antioch. We are going to see unusual works of God, as Paul did in Ephesus. If we embrace a genuinely apostolic ethos, there is going to be a release of signs, wonders and miracles. There's going to be handshake evangelism and napkin miracles – and so much more besides!

Ordinary People, Extraordinary Power

Reading this, it could be that some will feel that I am only talking about the individual and well known apostle, such as Paul. Actually, I am not. I do not personally believe that this kind of ministry is going to be the sole preserve of high-profile Christians. Actually, I sense more and more that God is going to use the kind of people we read about in Acts 11:19–21 – people with no famous names. It's actually interesting to my mind that the names of the Antioch Christians who were so radical in their pioneering mission are not recorded by Luke. The hand of the Lord was with them – but we are not allowed to know who is referred to by the word 'them'. God's powerful hand was upon faceless people.

In the light of this it is vital to believe that the Lord can use you in ministering 'a touch from the King'. Many Christians are held back by an acute sense of personal unworthiness. They honestly believe deep down that the King's touch is something that can only be ministered by the great 'man of God', by the so-called 'superstars of Christianity'. In reality, the King's transforming touch is going to be ministered more and more through unknown believers. God's going to use ordinary people to do extraordinary things.

This struck me when a housewife wrote to me about how the Lord had been ministering through her in healing miracles:

> Around 18 months ago, I met a couple called K and S briefly at a party. They were non-Christians. Soon afterwards I heard that S had been diagnosed with cancer of the bowel. She was due to have an operation to remove it, and then begin chemo. K particularly was devastated by the news. I decided to write S a

note to say I would be praying for her. I asked the Lord what to write and He told me to put 'I believe the Lord will heal you of your cancer and you will both become Christians'!! Needless to say, I was very reluctant to send the card. I did, however, and a few days later S had the operation. When she came round, the surgeon said to her, I'm not sure what's happened, but we cannot find any trace of cancer. You definitely do not have cancer any more. Shortly afterwards, they both became Christians and are going on well with the Lord.

In January this year, I walked past a lady that I didn't know, who wasn't a Christian, and the Lord gave me a scripture for her: Isaiah 61. I told her I was a Christian, and shared with her that the Lord wanted to give her the oil of joy instead of mourning etc, and she began to cry. She said that her brother-in-law had been in a motorbike accident and was on a life-support machine. His family were Jehovah's Witnesses and wouldn't let him have a blood transfusion, and the doctors had said he would probably die that day. I think around 90% of his bones were broken, and his organs weren't working.

I asked if I could pray with her, and prayed that before he died he'd become a Christian. I decided to take a step of faith and pray that he wouldn't die, but that there would be a miracle, so she would know that God is alive and cares about her. Later that night I received a phone call to say one of his lungs had started to work and the doctors were amazed. Soon afterwards he came round altogether and has now made a full recovery! A few weeks later the lady gave her life to the Lord; I'm trusting that her husband will also.

I'm sorry to go on for so long, but I'm really excited. I've just started running an Alpha course which is going great – all bar one have become Christians. The one who hasn't become a Christian yet is almost completely deaf and I'm looking forward to seeing him healed and converted on the Healing session in two weeks' time!

It is important to believe that God can use anybody in ministering his touch. You don't have to be a high-profile Christian. All you have to be is ready and obedient. God is looking much more for availability than ability in these days.

The Importance of Perseverance

Having said that, there is a cost involved in this kind of ministry. While apostolic Christians may see more of God's power, they will at the same time need to exercise more perseverance in the face of great challenges. Apostolic Christianity will not only experience a new appreciation of the Spirit. It will also experience a new appreciation of the Cross – both the message of the Cross and the marks of the Cross.

A Bible verse that has been stirring my heart for a long time is 2 Corinthians 12:12 (NIV). In these words Paul defines the very essence of apostolic Christianity. Speaking to the Corinthian Christians, Paul reassures them that he is a true apostle with these words:

> The things that mark an apostle – signs, wonders and miracles – were done among you with great perseverance.

Notice the word 'perseverance'. It is easy to miss that. We like the sound of 'signs, wonders and miracles'. We accept that these are the characteristics of an apostle and feel warm to the idea of praying 'More, Lord' in those areas. But we feel less warm about the idea of 'perseverance', the idea of exceptional patience and persistence in the face of big obstacles. It's one thing to pray for more power. It's another thing to pray for more perseverance.

When it comes to ministering the King's touch, both are needed. Sometimes, just one touch really does change everything. God moves mightily and instantly, and a mountain of difficulty is levelled in the twinkling of an eye. At other times perseverance is required. More than one touch is needed. We have to keep pressing in and persevering as we pray for the royal touch of heaven in a needy person's life.

And all this is consistent with the ministry of Jesus. There is one occasion when one touch does not secure the complete healing of a person in great need – when perseverance is called for and a second touch is needed. This is recorded in Mark 8:22–26:

> Then He came to Bethsaida; and they brought a blind man to Him, and begged Him to touch him. So He took the blind man by the hand and led him out of the town. And when He had spat on his eyes and put His hands on him, He asked him if he saw anything. And he looked up and said, 'I see men like trees, walking.' Then He put His hands on his eyes again and made him look up. And he was restored and saw everyone clearly. Then He sent him away to his house, saying, 'Neither go into the town, nor tell anyone in the town.'

Here is an exception to the idea, 'Just ONE touch . . . changes everything.' It seems that two touches were required in this instance. Notice, Jesus did not give up after praying once. Nor did he criticise the man for a lack of faith. He recognised the call to persevere and he pressed in for more. He was faithful.

Mahesh Chavda has written a book with a similar title to mine. His is called *The Hidden Power of the Believer's Touch*. He writes about the importance of perseverance:

> Be excited any time there is a change for the better when you touch someone in the name of Christ. I have learned to aggressively thank and praise God for any improvement, any miracle. This seems to set a pathway for healing. God is pleased when we are faithful – full of faith. Once you start touching people, stay in this path. Don't allow temporary setbacks to discourage you. I have learned that the healing touch is more an art than a science. Your persistence will accrue rich dividends.

And again, Mahesh writes this of his own journey of perseverance in healing prayer:

> When I began to see that when I laid hands on people, sickness withdrew, and pain disappeared, and when the blind started seeing and the cancers evaporated, I was excited. I knew I could not do it, but it was the virtue of the awesome King of Glory, Jesus Christ of Nazareth. With this excitement came

a passion to exalt Christ and make a difference through the laying on of hands. I learned that there could be setbacks from time to time, but the Lord's truth never changes. I learned in some circumstances to pray for a situation and pray again and again. As you extend the believer's touch, know that in some circumstances you may have to lay on hands every day. Sometimes the healing may be instant, and certain times you have to lay on hands many times.

Sometimes, ministering the King's touch requires great perseverance and persistence. It requires prevailing prayer. There are occasions when people do not receive the fullness of their healing at one particular time. Sometimes they need two touches from the King, not just one.

Take the following incident as an example. This is from a friend of mine called Nicky who lives in Australia. She received a remarkable touch from the King at a recent healing conference. She writes:

I have lived for many years with one leg shorter than the other. When I was sixteen years old I slipped a disc in my back and was unable to walk. It went again when I was eighteen, and after that I was in constant pain with my back every day of my life. Some days it was unbearable and others it was just a dull ache, but I took painkillers every day from when I first did the damage. It turned out that my back was not in good shape structurally as I had a deep curvature of the spine, twisted pelvis, one leg shorter than the other and scoliosis. I was told that I would have trouble in childbirth, wouldn't be able to dance again or run, and there was nothing the doctors could do for the condition.

When I became a Christian, at the age of twenty-three, I went to a healing seminar at St Andrew's Church in Chorleywood. At that meeting, God released me from the constant pain that I had been in since I was sixteen years old. Since then I have not had to take any painkillers, which, considering I had been taking them every day, was such a miracle and such freedom for me (I have had two children with absolutely no problems and I go running).

However, structurally, nothing had changed and my physio-therapist used to say that he couldn't believe that I wasn't in pain when my back was so obviously dodgy. He said that my back was worse than most seventy-year-olds he sees as patients.

Anyway, on the Friday night, the first session of the conference this year in Australia, the presence of God was so beautiful. We were caught up in worship, and I really was not thinking about anything to do with my back or short leg. Over the years, I have worn built-up shoes or a wedge inside my running shoes, day shoes etc., and I have got by okay that way because of course the pain has gone. However, as I was worshipping I suddenly felt God lengthen my shorter leg. I was so surprised as I really wasn't expecting it. A few days later I went for a run and my leg felt quite uncomfortable and I realised that I still had the wedge in my running shoe so I sat down at the side of the road and took it out and then it felt okay.

The reason I am writing to you now is that I have just been to my doctor today and asked her to confirm it. She asked the osteopath from the practice also to come in and they confirmed that my legs are both the same length and the pelvis is now not twisted.

Here is an example where perseverance was called for. Nicky received a touch from the King years ago at St Andrew's. Then she received another touch in relation to the same need years later in Australia. Nicky pressed in for more and received it.

Sometimes we need to persevere for another touch from the King. Sometimes there is unfinished business and we have to employ the PUSH principle – Pray Until Something Happens!

Another example is Julie Sheldon, whose testimony I shared in Chapter 2. Julie was dramatically healed of dystonia when an Australian preacher prayed for her in hospital. In spite of this there was some 'unfinished business' for her too:

One part of my body that wasn't made well was my left hand. The fingers stayed curled in a shape like a fist, and although it made carrying and holding things difficult the main impact was if my husband wanted to hold my hand. Instead of a nice flat palm he got a fist. It was an intimate thing between my husband and me and we didn't feel able to pray for it to be healed – it somehow felt churlish after the enormous restoration of the rest of my body! Then one day even that was to change.

I had gone to stay at Burswood to finish writing the book about my healing. It was a warm summer's day and I was sitting on the terrace overlooking the beautiful gardens and holding the finished manuscript on my lap. I experienced a profound sense of thankfulness for all that had happened and offered up a prayer saying as much, when an image came to mind.

This picture, in my mind's eye, was of a woman wearing a pretty dress surrounded by three groups of people. In my understanding of what was going on in the image, the healing I'd experienced was being likened to a gift, a gift of a new dress that was good and fitted well.

The first group of people were saying, 'What a pretty dress, how lovely it is – thank God for the healing that has taken place.'

In the second group a person was crying and weeping, saying, 'It's not fair. Why should you have such a pretty dress? Why should you be healed?' Another person was standing in the same group, looking really angry and accusingly muttering, 'It's not fair.'

The third group of people were lying sprawled on the ground, looking up at the lady in the dress and saying, 'Well, it looks very pretty to us. I bet there's nothing at the back. I bet the dress will fall down . . . I bet the healing will fall down and you'll be back in a wheelchair before too long.'

I think you could imagine how I felt perceiving this image, and as I looked more closely at the dress I noticed that the hem was unfinished and there was a thread hanging down on one side. Quickly I gathered up the manuscript and went off to try and find someone who might be able to help me understand this strange vision that had taken place. I bumped into one of the chaplains, who very wisely said, 'Let's go into the chapel and pray' and then proceeded to ask God to 'sew up the last bit of the hem'.

We didn't even get the chance to say 'Amen' because my left hand immediately sprung open – there was no sign of thickening of the ligaments and tendons – no nodules – only a smooth flat palm. It was amazing, incredible and instantaneous.

What has been even more intriguing about this image is that wherever I've had the privilege of speaking about this, there have always been these three groups of people present! Those

who say, 'Yes, I believe God still heals today.' Others who cry
and state accusingly, 'It's not fair, why should God heal you
and not others?' And of course there are plenty of people who
will say, 'Well you look fine, but give it a couple of years. You'll
soon be back in the wheelchair.' My response can only be that
I've been completely well now for seventeen years!

But what of the unfinished hem? God has used this picture
more times than I can say to encourage other people that he longs
to 'sew up' areas in their lives that need healing or resolving.

Julie pressed in for the fullness of her healing and received
another touch from the King. This completed the work
begun so powerfully in hospital weeks before. This is a great
encouragement to persevere. When we don't receive all that
we ask, we need to listen to the Lord and pray in the light
of what he says.

Keep Right on Till the End

These are days of power, when the Holy Spirit is clearly
moving in and through an increasingly apostolic church.
Miracles have been on the increase since the start of the
twentieth century. Ever since the outpouring of the Holy Spirit
at Azusa Street in 1906, God has been confirming the Gospel
with signs and wonders. The Good News that Jesus has died
to save and rescue us has been accredited time and again by
works of supernatural power. This has happened consistently
in the Pentecostal, Charismatic and neo-Charismatic moves
of God. It is on the increase again today.

At the start of this chapter I mentioned the remarkable rise
and growth of the Pentecostal churches. These churches have
always believed that the power of Pentecost is for today,
not just two thousand years ago. There is an old traditional
Gospel song that says it all for me:

Glory, glory, glory, somebody touched me,
Glory, glory, glory, somebody touched me,
Glory, glory, glory, somebody touched me,
Must have been the hand of the Lord.

While I was praying, somebody touched me,
While I was praying, somebody touched me,
While I was praying, somebody touched me,
Must have been the hand of the Lord.

Glory, glory, glory, somebody touched me,
Glory, glory, glory, somebody touched me,
Glory, glory, glory, somebody touched me,
Must have been the hand of the Lord.

It was on a Sunday, somebody touched me,
It was on a Sunday, somebody touched me,
It was on a Sunday, somebody touched me,
Must have been the hand of the Lord.

Glory, glory, glory, somebody touched me,
Glory, glory, glory, somebody touched me,
Glory, glory, glory, somebody touched me,
Must have been the hand of the Lord.

In this centenary year of 2006 I want to say that we owe a great debt of thanks to the Lord for pouring out his Spirit at Azusa Street in 1906. Since that time the Holy Spirit has been moving in ever stronger ways, restoring the miraculous to the contemporary church. These are truly days of power.

If these are days of power, they are also days of perseverance. As the saying goes, new levels bring new devils. The battle is on for the church to really believe the Bible, the Word of God. The battle is on to believe that God still saves, heals and delivers today. The battle is on for the Gospel – for the church to guard and proclaim the timeless truth of the finished work of the Cross. The battle is on and the battle is fierce, but in the midst of all the compromise and deception God is raising up a truly apostolic church. This church is the church through which the King of kings is going to minister his life-changing touch in ever-increasing measure. This church is the church through which revival will come to the nations.

Those who sign up to God's courageous, new, apostolic church will need to persevere. Perseverance will be necessary as well as power. God's call is for faithfulness – and not just faithfulness for a season, but faithfulness to the end. The great healing evangelist Smith Wigglesworth died in the vestry of his church just after preaching his last sermon. A letter was discovered in his pocket, addressed to his good friend Mrs. Helen Reid, wife of Pastor Andrew Reid of Scotland. Helen had been converted under the ministry of Welsh revivalist Evan Roberts when he had visited. Smith had also prayed for her son James, who was healed of cancer of the brain. Andrew and Smith were the closest of friends. This is how the letter reads:

From 70, Victor Road, Heaton, Bradford, Yorks.

March 11, 1947

My dear Sister in Jesus!

Many thanks for your letter received.

All saints are being tried. This is a proof that we are His, but we are more than conquerors through Him. The trial of your faith is more precious than gold tried in the fire.

On January 4th this year God gave me a real victory over a bad case of cancer. Early in the morning God gave me Luke 10:19, 'I will give you power over all the power of the enemy and nothing shall by any way hurt you.' I prayed for a very helpless case. Lost almost all flesh all strength (skin and bones, and without strength). She could not walk nor use her arms. The Lord's presence was so real. He Himself wrought a great miracle as soon as hands were put upon her – she was able to walk and use her arms and no more pain. About ten people came into the room and with one voice said, 'We have never seen anything like this before.'

You can understand what joy and presence of God filled the house. So you can just imagine what the house was like – full of joy in the Holy Ghost.

Smith Wigglesworth

These are days of power and they are also days of perseverance. To put it another way, they are days in which we are going to become more acquainted with the Spirit and more acquainted with the Cross. If we remain hungry for the power of God and faithful to the message of the Cross, we will see many instances confirming the truth that just one touch from the King changes everything.

Conclusion

When Everything is Changed

When people were touched by the King in the Gospels, it changed EVERYTHING . . . and the same is true today.

Just one divine touch can produce a dynamic zone in which a person's marriage, family, church and workplace experience the shock waves of God's amazing grace.

In the introduction I wrote about Hank. He shook my hand in a small church in Ohio. Unknown to me, God's power touched him with extraordinary results. For one thing, he was healed physically. For another, he gave his life to Christ. And even more amazingly, it affected his wife, his son, his church and his workmates on the construction site.

In fact, his wife Tina keeps on sending emails with the latest encouraging evidences of change. Take this one for example:

> Just a note to let you know what has been happening with Hank. It is really amazing the way God is working in his life. He has been speaking out to a lot of the men on the construction site about how Jesus has changed his life. He has invited several to church and they have come!
>
> He has joined the welcome team at our second Sunday morning service and goes up to church early to set up and clear up. We had baptisms two weeks ago and he said that he wanted to be baptised – and this from a man who a few months ago said, 'No way! I don't need that!'
>
> A friend of ours has a daughter who is fifteen and has a lot of problems. She has talked about being depressed. Hank went over to her house and told her about what happened to him

and she came to church with her family Sunday and will be coming back. Again, thank you for writing that note to him and being open to God working in your life.

And this one:

Near the end of our first Sunday service, a homeless man sat down behind us at the very back of church. We didn't see him come in. When the service was over, Hank started talking to him. It was obvious from the way he looked that he had fallen on hard times. Hank has an amazing gift that enables him to treat people from many walks of life with respect, dignity, and caring. He continued to talk to this man who he found out was named Keith.

Hank continued to talk with him. Hank asked him what he did and Keith said, 'Just walk – I'm just walking.' And Hank said to him, 'Brother, aren't we all. I am no different than you. A few months ago, I was just wandering with no purpose, and I came in here, and my life was changed.'

At one point Keith said, 'Maybe I should just leave. I am so disappointed in people.' Hank told him that he WOULD be disappointed in people – all people are disappointing, and that his hope would be found only in God. Then Keith said something about just leaving. And Hank told him, 'No. You've already come in here, the next service starts in 10 minutes, I suggest that you go back in and sit down for one more hour – what do you have to lose? Sit down and really listen, and see if you don't hear God talking to you. We'll pray and see what can be done for you practically.'

I believe that God put Keith behind Hank, because He wanted to use Hank to touch Keith. Hank showed him respectful mercy and treated him with dignity. It was awesome to see. If Hank hadn't spoken with him, he could have left without anyone knowing. I later found out that Keith did stay for the service and someone from church gave him a ride, and a hotel room for the night – a little slice of heaven to get a bed and a shower, done in Christ's name.

And this one!

The work God started in Hank is alive and well and thriving – and Hank is touching others and extending the Kingdom to even more people.

And not just this incident; he talks regularly to anyone who will listen about the difference God made in his life. He takes Pastor Van's sermon tapes to work and gives them out. He is even planning on every Friday having a pizza lunch on the construction site for whoever wants to come, and playing Van's sermon tape, so they can all discuss it after. A construction site is not the first place most people would think about discussing a church sermon. But Hank is so bold – he just does it.

I am so amazed when I look at him. He is NOT the same person he was for all of the 30 years I have known him.

You may think this is all just labouring a point – but the point must be laboured! When the King touches your life, everything changes. It is not just the area of your life that you thought needed touching – that sickness, disability, addiction or weakness. Everything is touched.

Are you prepared to let the royal touch of heaven transform everything in your life? Are you prepared to let the King's touch change your life so that you have to embrace a greater cost? Are you ready to let Jesus turn your disease into discipleship?

I meet people who desperately want the King to touch their lives, but on their own terms. That is not how it works. Jesus doesn't just want to be Lord over your health. He wants to be Lord over your family, job and leisure time too. If Jesus isn't Lord of all, he isn't really Lord at all.

I meet other people who have become so dependent on their disability or their sickness that they cannot let go of their need to be needed and their need to be noticed. They want the King's touch but they want also to hold on to their dependency. But that is not how it works either. There is only one healthy dependency – a total reliance on our All-Sufficient God. All other dependencies need to be renounced. We need to be desperate for him – and for him alone.

So, everything must change. That's the way it works. Jesus is the King of kings. When he reaches out his hand to you it is the hand of the King of kings and Lord of lords that touches you. This is no ordinary hand. This is no ordinary rule. God's rule will touch your life but EVERYTHING has to change, and this will involve cost. Are you prepared to count the cost? Are you prepared to let everything come under God's reign?

Hank's story is one of extraordinary, life-changing miracles resulting from just one touch of the King. The good news is that this can happen to you and me too if we are truly prepared to let God be God in our lives.

So stretch out your hand to receive a touch from the King today.

Then stretch out your hand to someone else, in the King's name, and release his love to them too.

Bibliography

Chavda, Mahesh, *The Hidden Power of the Believer's Touch*, Milton Keynes, Authentic Media, 2003

Sheldon, Julie, *Dancer Off Her Feet*, London, Hodder & Stoughton, 1991

Tolkien, J.R.R., *The Lord of the Rings*, London, HarperCollins, 2005

Turner, Daniel, *Art of Surgery*, public domain

Warren, Rick, *The Purpose Driven Life*, Grand Rapids, Zondervan, 2003

Prophetic Evangelism
When God Speaks to those who
Don't Know Him

Mark Stibbe

In this compelling book, Mark Stibbe argues that God wants to speak prophetically into the lives of unbelievers, waking them up to the fact that Jesus is alive and he knows their every thought, word and action.

There are many biblical examples of God's people using prophecy in their witness to unbelievers. Jesus used prophecy in his ministry to seekers. After Pentecost, God gave the gift of prophecy to believers as one resource among many in their witness to the world. Furthermore, Christians today receive prophecies for those who don't know Christ, often with immediate and life-changing effects. This book contains many such testimonies.

This is the first book to explore how the gift of prophecy can be used with potent effects in our outreach to non-Christians.

Healing Today
When the Blind See and the Lame Walk

Mark Stibbe & Marc A. Dupont

Do you wish you had more faith when praying for people to be healed?

One of the principal demonstrations of God's power is divine healing and it is happening more today than during the whole of church history.

Mark Stibbe and Marc Dupont confront the commonly held belief that spiritual gifts like healing ceased at the close of the apostolic era at the end of the first century. They believe that God still heals the sick today as we pray for them in the name of Jesus, and they share from what they have discovered about how healing functions as just one expression of the love of God.

The Father You've Been Waiting For

Mark Stibbe

It has been said that today's generation of young people – those in the 14–35 age bracket – are the generation of divorced parents, absent fathers and broken homes. More than any other in history, this generation is the 'fatherless generation'. Everywhere people are asking, 'where is the love?'

In this book, popular author and speaker Mark Stibbe answers that question by pointing to a story told 2,000 years ago by Jesus of Nazareth. The story tells of a father who demonstrates the qualities of a perfect dad. More than that, the story paints the clearest picture of what Jesus thought God is really like.

This book is a source of extraordinary hope for people of all ages and all beliefs (and indeed no beliefs). It provides a wonderfully accessible introduction to 'the Father you've been waiting for'. It also contains many new insights into a story loved by millions and known as 'the parable of parables'.

Passion for the Movies
When God Speaks to those who Don't Know Him

Mark Stibbe & J. John

Watching movies whether it be at the cinema, on DVD or TV is still amongst the most popular pastimes today. Everyone loves a good movie!

Many contemporary movies contain biblical values and principles that provide insights into in our lives and destiny.

Passion for the Movies examines 20 films and reveals the spiritual parallels that surface through each storyline. We hope these spiritual insights will be illuminating and give a perspective that is enriching and invaluable.

Each chapter also includes a 'questions' section to provide stimulus for discussion in a small group setting.